WINNING ATTITUDE

THE POWER OF
CHOOSING YOUR DESTINY

For more information on foreign distribution, call 717-530-2122.
Reach us on the Internet: www.soundwisdom.com.

Sound Wisdom
P.O. Box 310
Shippensburg, PA 17257-0310

Corporate Edition ISBN: 978-1-937879-97-6
ISBN 13 TP: 978-0-7684-1088-4
ISBN 13 Ebook: 978-0-7684-1093-8

Cover design by Eileen Rockwell

For Worldwide Distribution, Printed in the U.S.A.
1 2 3 4 5 6 7 8 / 18 17

Contents

PREFACE

Ram, a young man of 25, always shied away from hard work. Despite being born to a farmer, he tried his best to avoid working in the fields. His father was worried and displeased at his son's behavior, but he was resigned to the fact that there was nothing that could be done. He had tried all the tricks of the book.

One day, while Ram's father was working in the field, he fainted and dropped down. The family doctor was rushed in. He diagnosed that Ram's father had had a heart attack. Ram was worried sick. Two days passed, and his father was still in bed. On the third day, he called Ram and said, "Ram, the doctor has advised me bed rest. I cannot work anymore. The family is now is your hands. What do you plan to do?" Dumbstruck, Ram did not know what to say.

If you were to complete this story, how would you do it? Perhaps Ram's father gives him a magic stone that transforms him overnight into a hardworking, successful farmer.

Are you waiting for some magic to turn your life around in a day and the "aha" moment in your life that could solve all your problems too? Do you expect to read that you are at the right place, holding the right book that would enlighten you with the magic solution?

Don't be surprised—this book is none of that. It doesn't have any quick-fix solutions, and it definitely does not aim to solve your problems in a day.

The book underlines attitude. It doesn't implore you to be someone you are not. It simply tells you what you can achieve if you have the right attitude. It takes you on a journey from failure to success and everything in between. It also empowers you with the right tools to take charge of your life.

Each chapter deals with one attribute of the right attitude. In all these chapters, you will be able to find answers to three crucial questions:

1. What is it?

2. Why is it important?

3. How can I develop it?

HOW TO USE THE BOOK

The best way to use it could be to read the whole book first and then go back to the characteristics that you would want to improve in yourself. The book is designed so that you can refer to any chapter at any time.

If you feel you lack one or more of the characteristics that make up the right attitude, then rest easy and roll your sleeves up. This book gives you a step-by-step approach to developing and improving your life skills. If you feel you have all the characteristics, this book would still help you revisit them in the times you need them most, because even the best of us need reminding. Remember, improvement is an ongoing process!

A long time ago, there was a man who used to read one particular book again and again. When asked why he was reading the same book over and over again, he simply said, "With time, we forget."

Your life doesn't have to be ordinary anymore. Change your life.

Here is wishing you an extraordinary life. Get started. Get motivated. Happy winning!

Chapter 1

The Right Attitude—How Does It Matter?

*"If you can't change your fate,
change your attitude."*
—Amy Tan

THE QUITTER'S STORY

Sonya and Anita were friends from college. Equally hardworking, both took the same subjects, developed the same skills, and even aspired to achieve the same career goals—entrepreneurship. After graduation, Anita went on to secure a job. With hard work and a little something else, she quickly moved on to establishing a flourishing business that was her dream.

Sonya, on the other hand, had a difficult time securing a job. Even though she was as hardworking as Anita was, she could not achieve the level of success she aspired for. Frustrated, she quit her job to establish her own business. When her networking attempts failed and she could not gather finances for her business, she curbed her entrepreneurial aspirations and went back to a job, at a lower level than before.

So, what was it that Sonya did that made her quit? What did she lack that prevented her from achieving success? Rather, what was the something extra that Anita had and Sonya did not? *The right attitude.*

In every sphere of life, we see successful people and we see quitters. Quitters are of different kinds—from those who quit after the very first attempt to those who quit after trying umpteen number of times. However, what defines them is a single term—*quitter.*

We all know what happens to successful people; we have all seen them or at least heard about them. They become role models and their lives become success stories. Their triumphs are shared—as case studies, as biographies and motivational articles, as documentaries and books and even through the broken word of mouth. These stories go on to enlighten and inspire millions of people.

But where do the failure stories go? Even though we are motivated by the struggles of successful people and the challenges they overcame, somehow we choose to ignore the stories of the people who have failed. Their failure stories just fade away into oblivion.

Who needs the failure stories, you ask? Interestingly, the failure stories provide much more enlightenment than success stories, because they show you the missing piece, like the story of Sonya and Anita.

SO WHAT IS ATTITUDE?

We all know what *attitude* means. Haven't we often used the word in sentences like, "With that attitude, he isn't going to go anywhere," or "What's with her attitude?"

Try describing *attitude* in a line. Well, are you tongue-tied? What about the answers to these questions: Which political party do you think is the best? Should television content be regulated as well? What steps should the government take to combat inflation? Which movie deserves the Oscars this year?

Weren't those questions easier to answer!

You probably have strong opinions and beliefs about these and many such questions. These represent your principles and convictions and influence your behavior. Attitude is nothing but the expression of those beliefs, values, and feelings. It dictates how you respond to everyday situations and how you evaluate people, objects, events, and issues.

Attitude has three components:

1. Emotional—your feelings about people, objects, or events

2. Cognitive—your thoughts and beliefs about the subject

3. Behavioral—your behavior about the subject

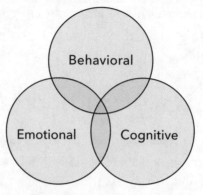

THE THREE COMPONENTS OF ATTITUDE

Did We Say a Clean Window?

To understand attitude, imagine it as a window through which you perceive the world. A constructive attitude is like a spotless window that allows you to see the world as it is and make pragmatic decisions to lead a productive life. Whereas a negative attitude is like a grimy window that lets through a hazy picture of the world and obstructs you from leading a meaningful life. George Bernard Shaw puts it better than anyone else can:

> *"Better keep yourself clean and bright; you are the window through which you must see the world."*

More often than not, people tend to use attitude in negative connotations. The examples presented earlier testify to this. However, attitude is more predominantly noticeable when it is positive.

Have you ever felt a vibrant aura when you are in the presence of successful people? "Wow, this guy has a great energy around him," you would have thought. Most times, the feeling lingers long after they've left the room.

This charisma or mysterious energy that you frequently associate with successful people is a manifestation of their exemplary attitudes. It is attitude that sets apart the mediocre from the majestic, the sparkling clean windows from the slimy ones.

Walt Disney had such a commendable attitude. When he was going to Hollywood to pursue his dream, he borrowed money and a suit from his friends and sold his camera to buy a first class train ticket, because he wanted to arrive in style! Despite being bankrupt and broke, he had vowed that if he was going to make it big, he was going to go first class all the way. He was extremely passionate about his dream and determined to provide the best quality in everything he or his company did.

William James, one of the celebrated thinkers of the nineteenth century, said:

> *"The greatest discovery of my generation is that human beings can alter their lives by altering their attitudes of mind."*

The first step toward altering our attitude is to understand the significance of attitude and to know our own attitude.

Why Clean Your Window?

What does a young entrepreneur envision when she starts her business? What does an established businessman endeavor for his organization? For that matter, what does every person work toward in life?

Success!

For every individual, the definition of success may differ. For an entrepreneur, success might be to make the best products/services available to the masses; for a writer, success might be to put into words the most complex feelings and emotions that define life; whereas for a manager, success might be to become a great leader, dynamically leading his organization toward its goals.

Even though success is what everyone wants from life and works toward, only a few achieve it. This is because success is a moving target; as we keep achieving one, we keep lifting the bar to form newer, higher goals. We are constantly looking to better ourselves, to go through the whole process and emerge at a level that is both satisfying and worthy. It is not an easy feat. Most of us lose our way somewhere along the road, while a handful others go all the way, breaking barriers and creating history.

Now wait a minute. Are you wondering, "Just now, we were talking about attitude, why are we now talking about success?" That's because there is a direct connection between the two. Thomas Jefferson states:

"Nothing can stop the man with the right mental attitude from achieving his goal. Nothing on earth can help the man with the wrong attitude."

Attitude is the first thing you notice about people and that people notice about you.

It is attitude that takes you all the way toward your success. If you look into the stories of people you admire, people you want to follow and people you wish to compete with, you will see that it is their attitude that differentiates them from the rest. One might argue that it is because of their successes that they have a great attitude. However, the reverse that is true—people become successful because they have a great attitude.

In addition to skills, technical acumen, and experience, attitude acts as a deciding factor in an individual's career. In fact, attitude is the precursor to success. If you look closely at the successful people in your life, you can see that their attitude fosters success. The right attitude attracts success. Dr. Joyce Brothers defines success beautifully:

"Success is a state of mind. If you want success, start thinking of yourself as a success."

IGNORANCE IS NOT BLISS

Despite the importance attitude has in our life, most people are not even aware of their own. Attitude acts at both conscious and subconscious levels. For instance, a person who is always niggling and complaining might not even realize that he is doing that! This is why it is important to look closely at ourselves and analyze our feelings, beliefs, and behavior to understand our attitude.

Here's an oft-repeated quote:

> *"There are three kinds of people. Some people make things happen. Some people watch things happen. And then there are those who wonder, 'What the hell just happened?'"*

Now, which category do you think the successful people belong to?

THE RIGHT ATTITUDE

A good attitude can make a bad day good, but a bad attitude can make it worse. What makes an attitude good or bad?

It is the little things that make a huge difference.

Think of a child who is learning to walk. In the gradual transition from crawling to standing up to walking, the child stumbles and falls umpteen times. What does she do after each fall? She gets up and tries again, and again, and again until she can walk without falling, each time with a smile and silent determination on her face.

What does the child not do? She does not give up after a few attempts, she does not drop down and cry, she does not try to blame the carpet or her parents or even herself for that matter, and she never stops trying until she achieves her goal.

Through this simple, natural process, a child teaches us the importance of the right attitude. A child is able to get up and try again every time, because her beliefs are not tainted with negativity and antagonism like ours are.

Sometimes, it is the little things that make a huge difference. You have probably never been bitten by a tiger or a lion, maybe by a dog, but most definitely by a mosquito!

The right attitude is a combination of these characteristics that may seem small or insignificant at the outset but make a huge impact:

- Dreaming high

- Being optimistic

- Being confident

- Having unwavering faith

- Being determined and passionate

- Building relationships
- Doing things differently

In the following chapters, we will look at each of these characteristics in detail. But we must learn to walk before we can run; before analyzing the attributes of attitude in detail, we must learn how to acquire the right attitude.

HOW TO GET A SQUEAKY CLEAN WINDOW

"A man, as a general rule, owes very little to what he is born with—a man is what he makes of himself."
—ALEXANDER GRAHAM BELL

Contrary to the popular belief, the kind of life that you wish to lead is entirely up to you. You have the power to overcome your adversaries and obstacles and emerge smiling from the most baffling situations and go on to claim victory.

Charles Swindoll said, "We cannot change our past. We cannot change the inevitable. The only thing we can do is play on the one string we have, and that is our attitude. I am convinced that life is 10 percent what happens to me and 90 percent how I react to it. And so it is with you...we are in charge of our attitudes."

Some people are born with great attitudes, some have an epiphany after a life crisis, while some have great mentors to guide them toward the correct path. But for most of us, the right attitude is a choice. Anyone can cultivate the right attitude, which is why it is unfortunate that one quits due to a lousy one.

FIGHT OR FLIGHT—TAKE YOUR PICK

If you don't believe that your attitude is your choice, let me tell you the story of John and Stephen, partners of a small, service-oriented business; let's call their company J&S Co.

Attitude is the reflection of your personality. Your attitude determines what and how much you can achieve.

In the initial stages after the inception of J&S, both John and Stephen were fiercely involved in acquiring and forming lasting relationships with their clients. Both would work long hours talking to prospects and working clients, holding brainstorming sessions with their co-workers and determined to become well known in their niche. Happy with their service quality, the older clients kept coming back, and a strong goodwill and smart advertising strategies got them a number of new clients. Slowly but steadily, they built their client base.

As J&S expanded, John started handling the clients, while Stephen managed their employees. With his optimism and passion, John soon built a reputation for himself among the clients, who enjoyed doing business with him. Stephen, hardworking and authoritative as he was, ably led his employees, who looked up to him, ensuring that every project was delivered on time. Together, John and Stephen made a great team. However, like every story that is worthy of telling, a problem issued forth in their case as well.

While everything seemed to be going well, the introduction of a new technology made the service offerings of J&S look obsolete. Just like that, J&S started losing their clients rapidly, as they preferred the cheaper and faster technology.

The company was in turmoil. They had to let several of their employees go, while several others quit to find opportunities elsewhere. They found themselves out of work on most days. Stephen started despairing; he stopped coming to the office and hardly spoke to his family, let alone John. He started preparing himself for defeat.

John, however, could not lose hope. He went to the office every day and was constantly researching for ways out of this situation. Eventually, the last employee, who had stayed back to help John, decided to quit as well, leaving John alone at the office. John felt he had two choices—to give up on his dream of becoming an accomplished entrepreneur or to stay on and fight for his dream. He eliminated the first one even before the idea materialized in his mind and set to work rescuing his company.

He didn't give up on his partner; through his constant support and encouragement and Stephen's own hardworking nature, he was able to instill hope and faith in Stephen.

Once Stephen was up and energetic again, they worked relentlessly toward finding solutions to overcome their obstacle, for that's how John saw it, and indeed, they arrived at the best solution that put them back in business.

The most important thing to notice here is that John had neither a mentor nor a miraculous vision; he simply had a choice. He chose to find other ways of redeeming his business rather than give up, and he did. The right attitude is as simple as a choice. There may be several things in your life that you cannot control—for instance, the fluctuations in market and people's responses to your products/services. However, you can control the way you react to all these situations. *Fight or flight, it will be your choice!*

Building the right attitude is like eating—you cannot do it just once a year!

Attitude is the manifestation of your thoughts and beliefs. Once you realize where you are going wrong, you are inevitably changing your thoughts. You then embark on a process of removing the dirt as it accumulates in the window of your attitude, making the sun shine brighter. In addition to that, when you read and listen to inspirational material, you start infusing constructive thoughts and values, polishing your window.

When you start weeding out unhealthy thoughts and inculcating positive ones, you start practicing a good attitude, eventually making it a habit. One of my favorite quotations of Mahatma Gandhi is:

> *"Your beliefs become your thoughts; your thoughts become your words, your words become your actions; your actions become your habits, your habits become your values; your values become your destiny."*

All you have to do is take charge!

CHAPTER REWIND

- Hard work alone is not the key to success.

- Passion, determination, faith, confidence, and a natural inclination to do things differently take you ahead in life.

- Right attitude is as simple as a choice.

- Developing a bad attitude is as easy as developing a good attitude.

- A constructive attitude is like a spotless window that allows you to see the world as it is and make pragmatic decisions to lead a productive life.

- Successful people have a great attitude. It is attitude that sets apart the mediocre from the majestic.

- You can cultivate the right attitude by weeding out unhealthy thoughts.

Chapter 2

DREAM...DREAM HIGH

"You will become as small as your controlling desire, as great as your dominant aspiration."
—JAMES ALLEN

KARAN AND HIS MAGIC PAPER

Karan was in eleventh grade. He knew that if not for his rich father, he would have never made it to eleventh grade. His grades had always been low. His teachers disliked him. Most of his classmates loathed him because he got away with his poor grades. He was a loner. But after his summer vacation, Karan promised himself that this year would be different.

During his summer vacation, he had visited his paternal grandfather. His grandfather had a soft spot for Karan, like all grandparents do, but he was also stern. One evening, his grandfather called him for one of his "talks" and asked him, "So Karan, how are you going to make me proud? What would you like to choose as your career path?"

All his life, Karan had hated the question, "What will you become when you grow up?" If someone ever asked him the ill-fated question, he would make sure that he/she was subjected to one of his infamous pranks. But he really liked his grandfather and was also a little afraid of his tempers. Karan thought it best to avoid the question by changing the topic. However, he was not successful at that. His grandfather was quite persistent.

Seeing he had no choice left, Karan burst out, "My dad doesn't care if I fail or pass; he has money and he will make sure I get the best. When I can graduate from high school without even turning a page, why should I bother?"

"Yes, I know your dad has money to buy you anything. Are you satisfied with that?" asked his grandfather.

"I know what I'm doing."

"Oh really? Then tell me, what exactly are you doing? Suppose your dad's business collapses overnight and he loses all the money. What then, eh?"

Karan looked at his grandfather dumbstruck. His grandfather continued, "Now that I have your complete attention, tell me, what would *you* like to choose as your career path?"

"I don't know," answered Karan finally.

"Hmm, I know you have been performing poorly at school and I know the reason for this too. But don't think you will have a chance of succeeding at your career simply because your father has money. If you don't have a dream, you don't have the drive to succeed. As simple as that. However, if you are satisfied with being a failure, you can continue doing what you have been doing so far."

This angered Karan. He did not like being a failure. Or did he? Even though his father's money had allowed him to progress in school, everyone he knew considered him a failure. And the worst thing was he hadn't done anything about it.

Smiling that he had got the kid thinking, his grandfather said, "Now is the time, Karan. You can still have your dream life you want. There is still a chance."

After a few hours of retrospection, Karan took an oath that he would turn his life upside down. Besides, his grandfather had given him a magic paper. He had asked Karan to read it whenever he felt low. He went back to school with renewed vigor and tried his best. Everyone noticed a change in him, but no one was ready to help him. However, Karan did not give up. Whenever he faced a mental barrier or any other setback, Karan would pull out his magic paper that grandfather had said would help him. The magic paper read thus:

> *"Thank you, God. I have graduated high school with wonderful grades. I have also been offered admission in the top universities for a course of my choice on my merit."*

Karan would look at this paper every day and read these lines to himself. Soon, his grades started improving slowly. Whenever he would falter, Karan would read the paper again. He wouldn't feel like reading it, but he would force himself to read it. The paper would instantly drive away dejection and make him feel motivated.

Karan had unknowingly stumbled upon a powerful tool of motivation. What he considered as a magic paper was actually the power of his mind. There aren't any magical papers lying around. Magic lies in your mind. Magic is the ability to weave out thoughts. Magic is to dream.

WHY FUSS ABOUT DREAMS?

This is the advice that every successful person gives us— *dream*. Well, we all dream when we sleep. It doesn't take much of an effort. Then why do these people keep telling us to dream, when it's so easy and everybody does it anyway? Perhaps they are talking about a different kind of dream. A.P.J Abdul Kalam, former President of India and scientist, wrote about this second type of dream in his autobiography, *Wings of Fire*:

> *"Dream is not that which you see while sleeping, it is something that does not let you sleep."*

Since the time we were children, we have faced one question constantly, "What do you want to be when you grow up?" Your answer to this question is your dream. It is how you see yourself in the future. You probably see yourself as a musician, an entrepreneur, a professor, a doctor, or a philanthropist. When you were young, you probably saw yourself as a combination of these. Some were even fantasies and unrealistic. But they were all your dreams.

Dreams require action to become true. Otherwise, they will remain just that—dreams.

Your answer to the question changes as you learn more—about the world, about yourself, your strengths, limitations, priorities, and the choices you have. As you grow up, you sieve your dreams and pick the one or two that seem the most possible. It is these dreams that have the chance of coming true. Dreams are the windows of possibility that your mind opens to you and calls you to pursue a path for its realization. As Walt Disney says: "If you can dream it, you can do it."

Dreams, then, of both kinds are not uncommon. If dreaming big can lead to success, then why do we not see a lot of successful people? It's because just dreaming is not enough. It's easy to say, "I want to be a movie star," but is it easy enough to become a movie star? Not really. Dreams require action to become true. Otherwise, they will remain just that—dreams.

MAGNIFYING THE LINE BETWEEN DREAMS AND GOALS

So, what should you do to make your dreams come true? Turn them into goals. There is a thin line between dreams and goals. The table below shows why dreams are intangible and goals are tangible:

DREAMS	GOALS
Dreams stay in dreamland.	Goals bring your dreams to reality.
Dreams don't have any specific outcomes.	Goals are based on predefined outcomes. They have a definite ending point.
Dreams are free. You don't even have to lift a finger to dream.	Goals require your time, effort, and other resources.
You can dream forever. Dreams don't have a time limit. Sometimes, people dream their entire lives, without ever realizing them.	Goals have deadlines. You either achieve them or form new goals. But you don't have the same goal forever; they would become obsolete after a period.
Dreams don't produce results.	Goals produce results—they actualize your dream.

EVER SEEN DREAMS WITH A TIMER?

Suppose you yearn to work close to nature. You love being outdoors and often see yourself as being out there and doing something that is related to nature. This is your dream, but not your goal. How do you turn this into a goal?

Goals are well-defined dreams with a deadline.

Add some specifics. It's all right that you want to work with nature, but what exactly do you want to do? A gardener, a beekeeper, a botanist/zoologist, wildlife photographer and journalist, a geologist—all these are professions involving nature. But there is a huge difference between each of them. So, what do you want to be? Once you decide that, you can then decide the time frame. If you don't set a deadline, you will never be motivated enough to start doing something to make your dream come true. Let's say you want to become a geologist within five years. Doesn't this seem much better defined than your dream?

HOW TO MAKE DREAMS TANGIBLE

Goals are nothing but well-defined dreams with a time limit. Here are the steps you need to turn your dreams into goals:

1. Pen It

Take a piece of paper and write your dream on it. This exercise is neither silly nor easy. Writing down something means you are committing to it. Elaborate as much as you can. Include as many details as you can see. We are not talking about a one-sentence dream here. It has to be the complete dream, as you see it and as you feel it. Ask yourself questions leading to the details until you see your dream as vivid and enthralling as a movie. Write these details down as best as you can.

Writing your dream also means that you are immortalizing it. This way, you are forcing yourself to think it through. It helps eliminate the vagueness of your dream and gives a value to it.

2. Specify It

Writing down your dream helps you specify your dream to an extent. But for giving a clear definition to your dream, you need to know everything about it. For instance, if you see yourself as an entrepreneur, learn everything there is to know about it. You may ask your friends, read books and articles, interact with entrepreneurs you know. Get as much information as you can. This will let you specify your dream, which would in turn make it more achievable.

For example, you can very well say that your dream is to become rich. But that is ambiguous; it calls for the following questions:

- How rich do you want to be—millionaire, billionaire, or multi-millionaire?

- How do you want to become rich? You can become rich by working harder and getting promoted in your current job, finding a job with a higher payroll, starting your own business, or even by winning a lottery. Unless you specify how you want to become rich, you cannot take the action required to become rich.

- When do you want to become rich—by the time you turn 30, 40, 50, or 60? This is crucial to determine the path you need to take to become rich. According to Parkinson's Law, a task swells in size based on the time frame set for its completion. For example, if you set a week to clean your apartment, it will take one week. But if you set aside one day, miraculously, you will find that you can clean your apartment in a day!

When you answer all the three questions, you are left with a goal. For instance, say you want to earn a million dollars per year by starting your own business by the time you are forty. Sounds challenging yet achievable, doesn't it?

3. Break It

Now that you have formed your goal, break it down into smaller goals. This is what makes your dream more real. It's easier to work backward on your goal. Just identify the logical steps to your goal, and these steps become your smaller goals. Forming smaller goals makes your dream more achievable.

4. *Plan It*

Form a plan of action for each of the smaller goals. This informs you of the course you need to take to make your dream come true. When you have a plan, start immediately. You can never wait for "life to settle." That never happens. If life settles, it is called death. If you need to achieve something and make your dream a reality, you need to get started right *now*.

Your dreams and aspirations determine how much of an effort you need to put in to achieve them. Stay steady with your dreams—be diligent.

> *"Too many of us are not living our dreams because we are living our fears."*
>
> —LES BROWN

A JUGGLING ACT—PERFORMANCE GOALS AND RESULT GOALS

Lina, a professional tennis player, was devastated. She had carefully formed goals that were achievable, created an action plan to help her achieve them, put in great efforts to follow the plan, and yet she did not win the crucial match she wanted to win so badly. As a result, instead of achieving the rank she aimed for, her rank went down several notches.

What was the mistake that Lina made? Let's take a look at the goals she had formed:

1.   Achieve improved ranking

2.   Win the crucial match

Do you see her mistake? If you don't see it yet, wait. Let us see Lina's opponent, Maria's, goals before that. Maria wanted to win too. But her goals were slightly different:

1.   Identify weak points in play

2.   Work on each to eliminate them

3.   Follow a practice schedule to improve play

Now, do you see the mistake in Lina's goals? Lina concentrated more on the results she wanted to achieve. When she was so focused on the results she wanted, she could not perform to her best, as she constantly feared the result.

Maria, however, did not focus on winning or losing. She concentrated on improving her performance. This not only allowed her to perform her best, but also resulted in her winning the match.

Result goals cause anxiety because you fear failure. This anxiety then prevents you from putting in your maximum efforts. That only makes you more depressed and frustrated. Performance goals, on the other hand, remove the anxiety of the result. They allow you to improve your skills, develop new skills and grow as an individual, and apply these to your action plan.

When you are not concerned about your result, you can give the task at hand your best. If you don't get the expected results, you can at least be satisfied knowing that you truly did your best. This knowledge allows you to get over failure quicker and strive again harder. However, if you did not get the expected result and if you did not give your 100 percent, it would only make you feel small. There is no shame in losing if you know you have done your best.

It does not mean that result goals are not important at all. Result goals are significant in that they show you your objective and make your progress measurable. So, how do you create your goals that balance result goals and performance goals? Make result goals your long-term goals, but make sure that your short-term goals are performance goals.

For instance, imagine you are the sales executive. If you set a result goal for your sales team—that is to achieve X sales by the end of the month—it is not likely to be achieved. However, if you break your result goal and set performance goals—to achieve maximum conversion each day—it is likely that the result goal would be achieved through the performance goal. If your team indeed achieves maximum conversion but fails to attain the result goal, then probably the result goal was out of sight!

AIMING HIGH BUT NOT OUT OF SIGHT!

You must have heard many times, "Goals must be out of reach, but not out of sight." What does this mean? This means that you should stretch yourself and aim high, but you should not make unrealistic goals.

Let's first discuss what unrealistic goals are. "I want to become Superman." This is not only unrealistic but also supernatural. Such feelings are wishes, desires, probably dreams. But they cannot be your goals, because they are unattainable. To get your dreams from the realm of fantasy into reality, your goals must be high enough to be achievable. Otherwise, your dreams stay as dreams. A more realistic and achievable goal in this case would be to say you want to be cast as Superman in a movie.

Suppose your goal is to lose 30 pounds in a month— that's pretty unrealistic, don't you think? Even if you go through the month giving your best and doing all you can, you cannot lose 30 pounds in a month. That will only make you feel disappointed and discouraged and would reduce your self-confidence. You would feel that you gave your best but could not achieve your goal. You would fail to see that this is only because you set an unrealistic goal. Moreover, if you know from the start that the goal is unattainable, you will not be motivated to work for it.

What are out-of-reach goals, then? You should set goals that are achievable, but *not below your capabilities*. Suppose a runner is capable of making 9- to 10-minute miles, which is the ideal time per mile for his age and build. However, he is too hesitant to take a risk and sets himself a goal of running a mile in 15 minutes. This he achieves easily and becomes displeased. This is because of the simple, unchallenging goal he set for himself. Columnist Maureen Dowd says:

"The minute you settle for less than you deserve,
you get even less than you settled for."

You may feel good about yourself initially when you set unchallenging goals. But constantly setting goals that are easily achievable only leads to dissatisfaction, displeasure, and in some cases overconfidence. Moreover, it does not give you a feeling of having achieved anything.

Let's say a student who is capable of scoring above-average grades constantly aims for a passing grade. Initially, a passing grade would satisfy her. However, as she would approach every test with the goal of receiving a passing grade, she would never realize her true potential. She would never know if she is capable of becoming a top scorer. This might lead to overconfidence, because for getting a passing grade she would not need to put in much effort. After a while, it would become her habit, and she would be plagued by discontent and disinterest, which would only affect her studies more.

More often than not, people set simple, easy goals because of the fear of failure. Like we discussed earlier, losing is not embarrassing if you know that you put in your maximum efforts. Besides, failure is a part of life. It only teaches us the right way to success. Mary Pickford, a Canadian actress, said:

"If you have made mistakes, there is always another chance for you. You may have a fresh start any moment you choose, for this thing we

call 'failure' is not the falling down, but the staying down."

If you set challenging goals, gave it your best, and failed, don't mind the failure and try again and again. At one point, you are bound to succeed. Remember that sometimes, when you are stretching yourself, you may fall short. But by all means, you would be doing much better than what you did when you set smaller goals. In the case of the student, if she aimed to score the highest grade instead of aiming for a passing grade, she might not always score the top grade. However, she would be scoring better grades than earlier. Apart from that, the satisfaction and the sense of achievement that you can feel after you achieve challenging goals would be priceless.

Set realistic, challenging, and achievable goals.

So, you should set realistic, achievable goals. But you should also aim high. How do you manage that? By knowing your strengths and limits and stretching yourself keeping those in mind. Don't be afraid to take risks, but make sure that the risk is not unworthy or unrealistic. Stretch yourself only to your strengths but not below your limits. So, in the case of the runner mentioned earlier, the ideal realistic and challenging goal would be to aim for a 6- to 8-minute mile.

This is not only within his limit and therefore achievable, but also challenging.

As British comedian Norman Vaughan said,

"Dream big and dare to fail."

NOW IS THE TIME

You have set the right goals for your dreams. You have formed your action plan. So, what do you do? Wait for the right time to start working on those plans? Wrong! No time is better than the present. You already have your dream, you already have your goal to make your dream come true; what are you waiting for? Start on the first step of your action plan today, this moment. But, simply in order to show yourself that you have started, don't do any activity that is not connected with your goal.

Fabre's Caterpillars

A French scientist named Fabre conducted an experiment with pine processionary caterpillars. These caterpillars are noted for their nose-to-tail procession—that is, each caterpillar follows the one in front. What Fabre did was to arrange a few of these caterpillars in a circle around a flowerpot and place pine needles (food for the caterpillars) just outside the circle. The caterpillars circled the flowerpot for seven days, but failed to get to the food and died of exhaustion and starvation in the end.

Though there is a perfect scientific explanation for what the caterpillars did, the point to learn here is that we would not get anywhere by doing just any activity. Would you simply take any flight when you have a destination in mind? You would take a flight that takes you to your destination, or at least near your destination. Similarly, when you have a goal in mind, don't consider any activity as an accomplishment. The only activities worthy of your time are those that would take you one step closer to the realization of your dream.

Any activity is not an accomplishment! Take one step closer to your goal with each activity.

Sometimes, all you need is a push in the right direction to get you started. Follow this simple activity; it is a surefire method for getting motivated. Take a piece of paper and write down what you want to achieve as if you have already achieved it. Read it as many times as possible in a day. It may sound silly, but it is highly powerful. These lines, though simple at first sight, are highly powerful. These let you know exactly how you would feel when you achieve your goal. This drives you more and more toward it.

As you move toward it, be sure to measure your progress periodically. This would bring you in line if you were deviating. But once you achieve your goal, don't fail to celebrate and don't fail to read your own paper where you wrote your goals. Rejoice in the feeling of satisfaction, because this is achievement in its purest sense.

CHAPTER REWIND

CHAPTER REWIND

- *"Dream is not that which you see while sleeping, it is something that does not let you sleep."*
  —A.P.J. ABDUL KALAM

- Turn your dreams into goals.

- Learn the act of balancing performance goals and result goals.

- Set targets that are achievable, but not below your capabilities.

- Not all activities take you closer to your dream.

Chapter 3

CHARGING UP ON OPTIMISM

*"The average pencil is seven inches
long, with just a half-inch eraser in case
you thought optimism was dead."*
—ROBERT BRAULT

YOU AND THE MAZE

Imagine yourself entering into one of those mazes with 8-foot hedges as walls and no cell phone reception. As you walk through the maze, you find that it is getting darker. You also find that there are obstacles in your way to prevent you from reaching the other end. As you near the heart of the maze (or so you think), it is so dark that you can only see a short radius around you with the feeble light from your mobile. Finding your way back to the entrance no longer an option, you have to keep walking on if you want to get out of the maze. Just when you take the next step forward, your mobile beeps, indicating a low battery alert.

Paints a pretty scary picture, doesn't it? Nevertheless, let's give it a try. Think of what you would do if you were stuck in such a situation.

If you were a pessimist, you would probably not have entered the maze in the first place. Even if you had entered, you would probably be thinking that you could not possibly get out of the maze, that no one would find you and that every bad thing in the world happens to you and you alone, and it was your bad luck that brought you to the maze.

Optimism lets you see the problem for what it is.

If you were an optimist, on the other hand, you would have a different approach to your situation—for what it is. Your thoughts would be focused on the solution, and you would be thinking of ways for getting out of the maze. You would analyze your position and evaluate your options. You might probably rummage your backpack and find a rusty old pocketknife in there. You obviously cannot carve your way out with that. What are your options? You could wait there until someone finds you or you could use your knife in some way to aid your escape.

You might then examine the hedge and find it to be strong and wide enough to support your weight. If you could carve out a couple of footholds in the hedge, you could get at the top of the hedge and find your way out or at least make yourself seen.

Did you see that solution before? If you were a pessimist, you would probably not. But if you were indeed an optimist, you would have believed that anything was possible. Every problem has multiple solutions. What allows you to see the solution is your optimism. When you indulge in negative thoughts, the voice in your head keeps telling you that you cannot achieve your goals and you are bound to fail, while trying to find fault with every opportunity that comes your way. However, if your thoughts are positive, you believe you can, which makes all the difference.

Coming back to the maze situation, having positive thoughts allows you to believe that you can get out of the maze; you just have to figure out a way. This allows you to focus on the solutions that might be lurking under the seemingly unsolvable problem. On the other hand, having negative thoughts makes you believe that you cannot get out of the situation, therefore obliterating your vision of possible solutions and forcing you to wallow in self-pity or loathing.

Every problem in life is like the stuck-in-the-maze situation; it's just a situation.

THE POWER OF "I CAN"

Everyone has heard about the half-full glass. Optimism or positive thinking is the first and foremost characteristic of a successful person. With positive thinking you can eat an elephant, if you so wish to. There is a beautiful quote by Mahatma Gandhi that emphasizes on this power of positivity:

> *"A man is but the product of his thoughts. What he thinks, he becomes."*

Being optimistic does not mean that you do an ostrich and bury your head in the sand against the troubles and challenges in your life. Optimism just helps you look at your problems in a different, more productive way.

THE POSITIVES OF BEING POSITIVE

Researchers and psychologists have studied the effects of optimism and pessimism on our lives and found that positive thinking has several health benefits.

OPTIMISTIC WAY OF LIFE	PESSIMISTIC WAY OF LIFE
Low levels of stress	High levels of stress
Longer life span	Anxiety
Happy with life	Unhappy with life
Less prone to depression	More prone to depression
Better ability to recover/ overcome setbacks	
Better physical health	
Reduced risk of heart disease	
Stronger immune systems	
Better mental ability	

HEALTH EFFECTS OF OPTIMISM AND PESSIMISM

How often we have heard stories of people fighting against life-threatening conditions like cancer and AIDS, conquering death and pulling through alive and energetic with a fresh hope for life. The determination and courage to achieve such a feat stems from positive thoughts and the belief that they can.

Several people who have suffered from such incapacitating illnesses have said that they considered their illness a gift. They say that their illness taught them the value of life, importance of living in the moment, and their life priorities. Sometimes, they were amazed by their own power when they discovered the strength of their mental ability even amidst difficult situations.

There are no definite theories for the health benefits that optimists enjoy. Nevertheless, researchers say that a positive outlook is a coping mechanism—especially for patients with terminal illnesses—and allows one to use a solution-oriented approach without magnifying the problems. Optimism, therefore, helps you manage stress more efficiently and overcome challenges more effectively than pessimistic people.

A quote by Helen Keller nicely sums up optimism:

> *"Optimism is the faith that leads to achievement...no pessimist ever discovered the secret of the stars, or sailed to an uncharted land, or opened a new doorway for the human spirit."*

THE CATCH CALLED REALISTIC OPTIMISM

Having stressed the significance of optimism, we need to realize that optimism has to be employed judiciously. Let the story of Rahman explain this.

Rahman was a 17-year-old boy who was highly optimistic about his career and life. This positive thinking was cultivated in him by his mother, who refused to see the glass half empty. Rahman's optimism and sincerity always got him satisfactory grades in school, and he was an above average student, if not a top scorer. His grades gained him entry into a decent college in his chosen field of study.

Growing up and studying in the same locality, Rahman had always been surrounded by friends. He was not exposed to the real world. However, he had to leave his safe nest behind when he left for college—unwittingly, of course. He made several mistakes that any excited teenager could make, but he was optimistic that things would always turn out to be fine, and they did.

It was then that he was introduced through common acquaintances to a group of gamblers, luring innocent students for their money. Rahman did not know the group's true intention. Skeptical and hesitant, Rahman did not gamble at first; he just watched his friends bet their hard-earned money. A couple of his friends were lucky and won, but most of his friends lost all their money and started dropping out. However, curiosity and greed overtook him, strengthened by his positive outlook that he would not, could not lose.

Optimism has to be employed judiciously.

He started betting the money he earned from his part-time job. Initially, he won meagre amounts, which fed his rearing greed. Eventually, he started placing larger bets and started losing inevitably. Even then, he did not lose his optimism and started borrowing money in the hope that he would win the next time. The "next time" never came. His friends started avoiding him because he had not returned their money and yet had not stopped asking them for more. He kept telling anyone who talked to him that he knew he would win big, and that he just needed some money to get there. He hardly attended his classes, his grades dropped, he lost his part-time job, and he was looked down upon by faculty and students alike.

When no one would lend him money anymore, he turned to his parents. He borrowed a large sum of money from them and placed them all in the hope of winning it all back. However, the group of gamblers took off with the money and never came back. Poor Rahman was so dejected that he lost his belief in positive thinking entirely and fell into depression.

What he failed to see was that his optimism was not the problem; the problem was the situation in which he chose to be optimistic. His optimism was unrealistic. When you have a positive outlook in unrealistic situations, your optimism will turn on you. It will only bring despair and disappointments.

Unrealistic optimism is just as bad as pessimism.

Instead, if you combine the positive outlook of optimism and the clear-eyed perspective of pragmatism, you will reap the benefits of both the worlds by becoming a *realistic optimist*. Sandra L. Schneider defines realistic optimism as follows:

> *"If we define optimism broadly as the tendency to maintain a positive outlook, then realistic optimism is the tendency to maintain a positive outlook within the constraints of the available 'measurable phenomena situated in the physical and social world.'"*

For constant improvement, certain things have to be challenged. Just thinking that everything is going to be fine will not elicit progress. For instance, you cannot clear an exam without any preparation just by thinking positively that everything will turn out to be fine. This is similar to staying in a crime-prone area but refusing to take necessary safety precautions thinking that no negativity would touch you.

9/11 AND J. P. MORGAN

To be a realistic optimist, you should know your strengths and shortcomings. You should see things for what they are and prepare accordingly, like J.P. Morgan, the financial giant.

When the World Trade Center was bombed in 1993, Morgan realized that the prestigious building they occupied was also a prime target for terrorism. He acted strategically and implemented escape drills in which all his employees took part actively.

Nine years later on 9/11, the terrifying attacks on the iconic twin towers took place, killing nearly 3,000 people. Morgan Stanley office was located in the south tower, which was second to be struck. The first tower was struck at 8:46 A.M. By 8:47 A.M., all 2,700 employees of Morgan Stanley were evacuating. The offices were nearly empty within 15 minutes. Even though their offices received an almost direct hit, they lost only seven employees. It was realistic optimism that saved the lives of 2,693 employees of Morgan Stanley.

Martin Seligman, the father of contemporary positive psychology, said in his book, *Learned Optimism*:

> *"What we want is not blind optimism but flexible optimism—optimism with its eyes open. We*

must be able to use pessimism's keen sense of reality when we need it, but without having to dwell in its dark shadows."

By being a realistic optimist, you can be motivated by both the power of optimism and the opportunity-seeking component of realism. This would pave the way for constant improvement.

CULTIVATING OPTIMISM? OF COURSE THAT'S POSSIBLE

"Cultivate optimism by committing yourself to a cause, a plan, or a value system. You'll feel that you are growing in a meaningful direction which will help you rise above day-to-day setbacks."

—ROBERT CONROY

We already saw in the first chapter that right or wrong attitude is only a habit. The same applies to optimism. In fact, Seligman provided scientific foundation to prove that optimism could be learned and cultivated as a habit.

Optimism can be learned just like any other skill.

For testing the concept of "learned helplessness," Seligman conducted several interesting experiments. One of his experiments consisted of applying mild electric shocks to two groups of dogs. The first group was provided with a lever, which when pressed could stop the shocks. The second group was also provided with a similar but dummy lever that did not stop the shocks.

Further, the dogs from the second group were wired to the first group, so that they received shocks of identical intensity and duration. This meant that when a first-group dog pressed the lever, it would also stop the electric shocks for a second-group dog wired to him.

Dogs in the first group quickly learned that they could end the pain and coped better with the situation. Dogs in the second group, however, thought that they could not stop the pain whatever they did. To them, the pain stopped randomly and the situation provided no escape. They started showing depression-like symptoms.

In the second part of the experiments, the same groups of dogs were placed in shuttle-boxes, which were designed so that they could escape from the shocks if they jumped over a low divider. Dogs from the second group simply lay down and whined, as they had learned from the previous experiment that they could not escape the pain no matter what they did. Dogs from the first group found the way out and hence escaped the pain. Even though all the dogs had equal opportunity to escape from pain this time, dogs who had learned to be helpless did not even try.

Similar experiments were conducted on people with noise instead of electric shocks and buttons to shut off the noise. Even in this case, Seligman found that when people had learned that the noise would not stop no matter which button they pressed, they did not even bother to try.

However, in the case of dogs as well as people, Seligman found an anomaly. One in three people would just not give up. They kept trying different buttons, attempting to shut the noise off. This intrigued Seligman, and he applied this question to real life: What makes some people pick themselves up after failures and try again and again until they achieve their goals?

He found that it is not just human will that lets people achieve this. This trait of never giving up was not something that is inborn; this was the result of optimism. Seligman found that optimism could be learned just like any other skill.

Positive thoughts arise from self-talk, which is nothing but the endless stream of thoughts that inhabit your mind every day. When your self-talk is positive, you are optimistic; when your self-talk is negative, you are pessimistic. Some of your thoughts originate from logic and reasoning, while some originate from your perceptions, judgments, and interpretations. It's the self-talk of the latter type that instils negativity and leads to stress.

SO WHAT'S YOUR TYPE?

Charlie Chaplin once said:

"You'll never find a rainbow if you are looking down."

Identifying negative thoughts is the first step toward developing a positive attitude. So, how do you find out whether your thoughts are positive or negative? It's not easy to analyze yourself, especially because you are bound to be prejudiced. However, self-analysis is much better than being told by someone else that you are pessimistic. Let's find out whether you have positive or negative thoughts dwelling in your mind through an exercise.

Suppose you are given the responsibility of a difficult project at your work. You work hard, motivate your team, put in extra efforts and time, and deliver the project on time. Both your clients and managers are extremely pleased with your work and praise you. However, one of your colleagues spots a minor mistake in your work. How would you react? Take a paper and compare with the two sets here:

Set 1

- "Why did he have to spot the mistake now? He just wants to show off and pull me down."

- "I can never get anything right, I always goof things up."

- "Why does stuff like happen only to me?"

Set 2

- "I am overworked."

- "I haven't been as careful as I usually am."

- "I am glad my colleague spotted the mistake, instead of the client."

Are you able to see the difference between the first set and the second set? In the former case, your thoughts are affected by negativity. You are unable to accept the fact that there is a mistake in your project, which cultivates feelings such as anger, self-pity, and depression. But in the latter case, you agree that the mistake has been made, which would in turn allow you to rectify your mistake and learn from your experience.

Whatever your way of thinking may be, it has a significant impact on the state of your mind. Interpretations like the former case, where you take the blame on yourself, suggest that you are incapable or you lack talent. This indicates that your misery is permanent, which leads to guilt and despair. However, in interpretations like the latter case, your reasons suggest that your misfortune is temporary and that it is not your fault. This prevents you from shouldering guilt and allows you to focus on the next step forward.

WHITE OR BLACK?

When you are a pessimist, you tend to think the worst of everything, magnify every problem, always blame yourself, and polarize everything—meaning you see either white or black; there's no grey area for you. Being an optimist allows you to see the bright side of things, thereby allowing you to visualize the results you wish to achieve. This in turn builds the confidence to accomplish your goals, and success follows just like that. As Abraham Lincoln said:

> *"We can complain because rose bushes have thorns, or rejoice because thorn bushes have roses."*

Psychologists say that being positive allows you to be resilient and be more engaged in what you do. This allows you to take more risks and handle difficult things with ease, which increases your productivity and ultimately your happiness.

Once you identify the nature of your thoughts, you can keep them in check when you are becoming too pessimistic or too unrealistic. Whenever you face a problem, take a moment to analyze your situation. Your problem might feel like the end of the world to you. But understand that there are millions of people who are thinking the same thing. If Armageddon arrived every time anyone thought that, we might not be alive right now.

When you analyze your situation closely, you might find that it's not so bad after all. Yes, some things seem unmanageable. But hey, you are still alive and kicking! As Dr. Seuss said:

> *"Don't cry because it's over, smile because it happened."*

Besides, imagine what a great story it would make to tell your friends and kids about how you overcame this problem.

Now look at your situation again; you're sure to find a way around it to emerge successful from it.

BEWARE! THESE ARE CONTAGIOUS

Do you know anyone who is pessimistic or depressed? Have you noticed that around them you start feeling uncomfortable? Negative people suck the energy out of those around them. Even one negative comment from a pessimistic person can ruin your best day.

However, the converse is also true. Your optimistic thinking can be a source of great positive energy to your environment and those around you. Every person affects and is affected by the people he/she meets. This happens instinctively at a subconscious level. Your words, thoughts, attitude, and body language have a great impact on the people around you.

Therefore, it's not just enough that you filter your negative thoughts and practice optimism; you have to make sure that you surround yourself with positive people.

THE OPTIMIST CREED

The optimist creed was written by the New Thought leader, teacher, and prolific author Christian D. Larson in 1912.

Promise Yourself:

- To be so strong that nothing can disturb your peace of mind.

- To talk health, happiness, and prosperity to every person you meet.

- To make all your friends feel that there is something in them.

- To look at the sunny side of everything and make your optimism come true.

- To think only of the best, to work only for the best, and to expect only the best.

- To be just as enthusiastic about the success of others as you are about your own.

- To forget the mistakes of the past and press on to the greater achievements of the future.

- To wear a cheerful countenance at all times and give every living creature you meet a smile.

- To give so much time to the improvement of yourself that you have no time to criticize others.

- To be too large for worry, too noble for anger, too strong for fear, and too happy to permit the presence of trouble.

CHAPTER REWIND
CHAPTER REWIND

- Positive thoughts keep you focused on solutions instead of problems.

- Optimistic thoughts have several health benefits.

- Unrealistic optimism is dangerous. Instead, aim for realistic but flexible optimism.

- Being positive allows you to be resilient and be more engaged in what you do.

- Positive attitude allows you to take more risks and handle difficult things with ease, which increases your productivity and ultimately happiness.

Chapter 4

Developing the Right Amount of Confidence

"Somehow I can't believe that there are any heights that can't be scaled by a man who knows the secrets of making dreams come true. This special secret, it seems to me, can be summarized in four Cs. They are curiosity, confidence, courage, and constancy, and the greatest of all is confidence. When you believe in a thing, believe in it all the way, implicitly and unquestionable."
—Walt Disney

BILL AND THE RICH MAN

Bill came from a middle class family, where no one had ever been an entrepreneur. This was probably why Bill had always been interested in being his own boss. As he grew up, he discovered his interest in automobiles. He dreamed of starting a company connected to automobiles in some way. After graduating, Bill decided to set up an automotive and assembly business.

However, building an organization is not easy and Bill had to start everything from scratch. After months of research, he prepared a proposal to arrange the capital his business required. He approached several investment banks with his proposal. After many rejections, two banks agreed to invest in his venture. He started his company with a determination and vigor to make it big.

Initially, he faced several challenges, but he had gathered a great team who worked together to overcome the setbacks. Gradually, he started paying off his loans. Things were going smoothly for a few years. He was looking to start making profits by large margins when he acquired a large contract from a leading company.

However, a technical error resulted in the loss of the contract. Even then, Bill wasn't dejected. He thought he would be able to pull it together. But seeing the leading company withdraw, the other companies that had agreed upon contracts also withdrew. This resulted in a huge loss for Bill's company.

Getting a whiff of the setbacks he was facing, his banks started pressuring him. On the same day, his suppliers came to him demanding payment. Deep in debt, Bill saw no way out. It was one of those days for Bill when nothing seems to go right.

Completely at a loss, Bill took a break and started walking aimlessly across the city. He came across a park and sat on a bench, head in his hands, wondering if anything at all could save his company.

Just then, an old man walked up to him and said, "What is the matter? You look troubled."

When Bill recounted his story, the old man said, "I believe I can help you."

The old man took a checkbook from his pocket and, asking Bill his name, wrote out a check. The man then pushed it into Bill's hands, saying, "Take this money. Meet me here exactly after a year. You can pay me back then." The old man then went his way before Bill could say anything.

Stunned, Bill looked at the check and saw it was for a whopping half a million dollars. What was more, the check was signed by Martin Drew, a name Bill recognized as one of the richest men in the city at that time! Bill thought that all his monetary problems could be solved with that money.

However, Bill did not cash the check. He decided to try one more time before cashing it and so kept the check in his safe. With renewed optimism and the confidence that if anything failed this time he had the check to save him, he met several clients and negotiated deals. He also went to the company that had first withdrawn their contract and reassured them of the highest quality and value for their money. With their contract back in hand, he went to his banks and asked for more time. He convinced his suppliers and motivated his employees.

Within a few months, Bill's company had secured more contracts than they had acquired since inception. And a few months later, Bill had paid off his loans and had started making profits.

After exactly a year, he went back to the same park with the intention of returning the check and thanking Mr. Drew for his timely help. At the agreed-upon time, Bill saw the old man approaching him. Before he could reach Bill, however, a nurse came running after him, reprimanded him for "running away again" and started taking him back. Puzzled, Bill quickly went to the nurse and asked her what it was all about and if he could have five minutes with Mr. Drew.

The nurse started laughing, puzzling Bill even more. The nurse then explained that the old man was not Martin Drew as he thought. His real name was David Andrews and that he was suffering from a peculiar amnesia. He often escaped from their facility and told anyone he met that he was Martin Drew and that he was a millionaire. Astonished, Bill asked the nurse how he came across the name of Martin Drew. The nurse said that it was just a coincidence. The old man did not know the real Martin Drew. His middle name was Martin and he shortened his last name to Drew. So saying, the nurse led the old man back to the facility.

Bill was more astonished than the last time he met the old man. He had spent the last year negotiating deals and taking risks he would not have taken otherwise, thinking that he had safe money to fall back on. He suddenly realized that it was not the money that had turned his situation around. The knowledge of the money had given him back his self-confidence to go after what he wanted. The money had just acted as a catalyst that had revoked his confidence. He returned to his office, promising himself that he would never lose his self-confidence again. He never broke his promise.

Finding self-confidence can be difficult, but without self-confidence finding success is also difficult.

HAND IN GLOVE: CONFIDENCE AND SUCCESS

Suppose you are taking a friend of yours to see a doctor for a serious problem. The doctor looks at your friend's case history and performs a basic examination. But all the while, the doctor seems jittery and seems to do everything twice, like checking the pulse twice, and so on. Then, he turns to your friend to explain what he thinks is the problem. He keeps using phrases like, "I think the problem is..." and "I'll show your case to my superior to confirm...."

After this, he starts writing out a prescription. Suddenly, he gets up, takes a huge book, and consults it muttering to himself, "Yes, of course...." He scratches out what he had written and prescribes a different drug. He checks it with the book again and then hands it over to your friend. Is your friend likely to take the drug the doctor prescribed? Would you let your friend take the drug?

Such is the impact of confidence on people. Or rather, such is the impact of low self-confidence. The above scenario of the doctor lacking self-confidence is just an example to emphasize the importance of confidence. The example of a doctor was chosen because of the magnitude of the profession. You can imagine any such scenario in personal or professional life. Confidence or lack thereof has a huge impact.

Right from the calm self-assurance of a doctor and the firm authority of a teacher to the charisma of a motivational speaker, it is confidence that we expect and confidence that we admire in people we look up to. Self-confidence is a crucial aspect of our lives. It is reflected in everything we do. When you exude self-confidence, it becomes evident not just to you but to people around you. The reverse is also true.

In *Peter Pan*, James M. Barrie wrote:

> *"The moment you doubt whether you can fly,*
> *you cease for ever to be able to do it."*

A self-confident person has a higher probability of making it big in his/her life than people who doubt their own abilities. Have you ever read about a successful person who was not confident about his abilities or ideas? Self-confident people have also been found to be more optimistic than people who are not confident of themselves. Fear of failure is your worst enemy. When you think you cannot succeed, you doubt your own abilities and hesitate to take risks, fearing failure. This would only result in you fulfilling your own prophecy.

Instead, when you believe you can, you will not be shaken by failures and you will not rest until you achieve your goal. We saw how determination is the harbinger of success. Confidence in your abilities is what drives you to be determined.

When you lack self-confidence, you start becoming pessimistic. You fear failure so much that you stop stretching yourself. If Bill had not found the old man in the park, he could never have turned the situation around so fast. He would never have had the guts to approach the company that withdrew their contract. Low self-confidence and fear of failure would not have allowed him to recover from his situation.

Self-confidence or the lack thereof has a huge impact on success.

Dr. Norman Vincent Peale, a progenitor of positive thinking, said:

"Without a humble, but reasonable, confidence in your own powers you cannot be successful."

Finding self-confidence can be difficult, but without self-confidence finding success is also difficult. It's a vicious cycle. If you have self-confidence, you can lead a successful life with enthusiasm. People trust you and respect you for your confidence. This in turn builds your confidence and the cycle continues. But remember, the cycle also spins in the opposite direction.

Self-confidence directly affects your success because it:

1. Allows you to stand up for what you believe in.

2. Lets you stand up for yourself when you are treated unfairly.

3. Helps you say no when it's necessary.

4. Allows you to say yes when opportunity knocks.

5. Helps you overcome the fear of failure.

6. Drives you to raise the bar and aim high.

7. Allows you to stretch your limits and take worthy risks.

8. Pushes you to ask questions at the right time even when others are silent.

HOW CONFIDENT ARE YOU?

How do you find if you have the right level of self-confidence? Self- confidence is reflected in your behavior, your body language, what you say, how you say it, and in everything you do. You can observe some basic differences in character traits in people with self-confidence and people who lack self-confidence.

You can match you behavior in the table below and find out for yourself whether you are a self-confident person.

A PERSON LOW IN SELF-CONFIDENCE		A SELF-CONFIDENT PERSON	
Behavioral Patterns	Check the box if this person is you	Behavioral Patterns	Check the box if this person is you
Has poor body language and seldom makes direct eye contact, especially in confrontations		Is poised and relaxed, has a confident demeanor, good body language, and always makes direct eye contact	
Acts based on what other people think		Does what he/she believes is right, regardless of how others may react/respond	
Often creates unrealistic goals and becomes disappointed when unable to achieve them		Creates high but realistic goals and strives to achieve them	
Fearing failure, never executes his/her plans		Puts his/her plan into action	
Performs within the comfort zone and avoids taking risks		Knows how much to stretch out of the comfort zone and takes calculated risks willingly	

A PERSON LOW IN SELF-CONFIDENCE		A SELF-CONFIDENT PERSON	
Behavioral Patterns	*Check the box if this person is you*	Behavioral Patterns	*Check the box if this person is you*
Covers up if he/she makes mistakes, hoping they wouldn't be discovered, and when discovered tries to blame someone else or the circumstance		Admits if he/she makes mistakes, and is willing to learn from and rectify them	
Does not have confidence in himself/herself and never volunteers for anything; work has to be forced upon		Believes in his/her abilities and volunteers for work accordingly	
Proclaims his/her accomplishments to as many people as possible		When he/she accomplishes something, waits for others congratulate	
Shrugs away from or dismisses compliments, for instance, "That project was nothing. Anyone could have done it."		Accepts compliments gracefully, for instance, "Thanks, I really worked hard on that project. Thank you for recognizing my efforts."	
Total Boxes Checked Column A		**Total Boxes Checked Column B**	

Remember: It is time to change if your score is anything but a zero in column A! Take the self-confidence test intermittently to keep checking your progress.

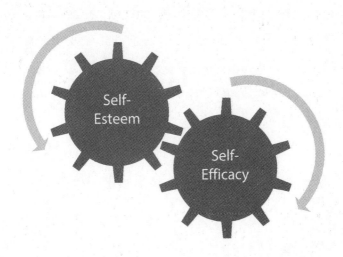

CAN YOU DEFINE SELF-CONFIDENCE?

Before looking at ways to build your self-confidence, let us look at what exactly self-confidence is. Self-confidence has two parts—self-esteem and self-efficacy. To improve your self-confidence, you have to work on both your self-esteem and self-efficacy.

PARTS OF SELF-CONFIDENCE

1. *The Outer Angle: Self-Esteem*

Self-esteem is how you think of yourself based on how you see yourself. It is the overall sense of your personal worth or value. Do you regard yourself to be valuable to others, or do you think you are not worthy of your society? Self-esteem is how you appraise your appearance, your performance in your personal and professional life, your beliefs and emotions. Robert Kiyosaki, author of *Rich Dad, Poor Dad*, says:

> *"It's not what you say out of your mouth that determines your life, it's what you whisper to yourself that has the most power!"*

Self-image fuels self-esteem.

A high self-esteem is important for you to grow as an individual. Only when you have a high regard for yourself will you have the confidence and the drive to succeed. People with low self-esteem will never try to realize their full potential. They will always think themselves unworthy and incapable.

Everyone has a self-image. It is based on this perception of themselves that people build their self-esteem. Our self-image is directly proportional to the quality of our life. In order to improve the quality of our life, therefore, we have to improve our self-image. As we improve our self-image, our self-esteem will enhance.

Suppose there is an auto-rickshaw driver who has never aspired to be anything else. He is so constrained that he has accepted his self-image and accepts that he never will be anything else. If he were given the opportunity to drive a Mercedes Benz car, his first action would be to search for the handbrake to start the car. This is because of the low self-image he holds of himself.

Self-esteem is also affected by whether people around us approve of us. Even though what people think of us is not in our control, we can change this by changing our self-image.

2. The Inner Challenge: Self-Efficacy

Self-efficacy is the belief that we are skilled in what we do and that we have the abilities to succeed in a given situation. It is the faith in our own abilities. People having a high degree of self-efficacy believe that if they were given the opportunity to learn a particular subject, they will be able to work hard and succeed. Self-efficacy is the most important part of self-confidence. It plays a major role in how you approach your tasks, goals, and challenges.

Faith in your abilities builds self-efficacy.

On the other hand, people having a poor sense of self-efficacy are unsure of their own abilities. They view difficult tasks as personal threats, which is why they shy away from challenges. They don't believe that they have the ability to handle difficult tasks. They have low aspirations and are not committed to the goals they set for themselves. They concentrate on their failures and negative outcomes. Minor setbacks pull them down, and they are disappointed easily.

Self-efficacy also affects your creativity and your ability to come up with ideas to solve problems. People with high self-efficacy believe that they can solve any problem they face. This in turn fosters creativity. People with a weak sense of self-efficacy curb their ideas even before considering them, which has a negative impact on their creativity.

Sylvia Plath, a poet and novelist, wrote in her book, *The Journals of Sylvia Plath*:

"The worst enemy to creativity is self-doubt."

BUILDING THE ARMOR OF SELF-CONFIDENCE

"Believe you can and you are halfway there."
—THEODORE ROOSEVELT

Developing self-confidence takes time, but it is not unachievable. Nevertheless, self-confidence can also be faked. Faking a brave exterior will help you get through a number of difficult situations. It also has the benefit of expanding your comfort zone. Moreover, when you overcome a situation like this, the fact that you were able to overcome the situation, even though you did it by faking confidence, will actually boost your confidence.

However, you cannot simply fake it in all situations. You are putting yourself through a constant fear of being found out. There is also the problem when you overdo it.

For instance, if you embellish your qualifications for a job and someone hires you, you feel constantly threatened. In some situations like this, it's just not worth faking it.

THE TEN-STEP GUIDE FOR BUILDING SELF-CONFIDENCE

Like they say, the original is always better than a copy. Let's look at these ten steps that build self-confidence:

1. List Your Achievements

Reflect on your life and think about all that you have achieved so far. List those that you consider the best. Probably, you were appreciated for your role in your team, or perhaps you aced an exam or delivered a project on time. Preserve this list and update it when required. Look at it from time to time and enjoy the success you have had.

2. Chart the SWOT

"Know yourself and you will win all battles."
—Sun Tzu

Go ahead. Draw four boxes, one each for your strengths, weaknesses, opportunities, and threats. Look at who you are and where you are in your life. Review the achievements you listed and jot down what you think and what your friends consider are your strengths and weaknesses. Think about the opportunities in your life and the threats you face. Make sure that you reflect on your strengths and opportunities and feel good about yourself.

3. Set Your Goals

Think about where you want to be and who you want to be. You can use your SWOT analysis and set goals that leverage your strengths, exploit your opportunities, lower your weaknesses, and minimize threats. Set yourself both personal and professional long-term goals and break them down into short-term goals.

4. Hone Your Skills

Now that you know where you are and where you want to be, list the skills you need to develop in order to reach your goals. Look at ways you can develop these skills. Build your knowledge. If you think a course would equip you with the skills and provide you the necessary certification or qualification, then overcome your fear and enroll yourself.

5. Start Small

> "Having once decided to achieve a certain task, achieve it at all costs of tedium and distaste. The gain in self-confidence of having accomplished a tiresome labor is immense."
>
> —THOMAS A. BENNETT

Split your short-term goals in to small, achievable goals, and make sure you achieve them. Form a habit of setting goals, achieving them, and celebrating them. Don't set challenging goals initially, you might only get disappointed. Just get into the habit of achieving small goals and celebrating your achievement. Pile up your achievements little by little. Gradually widen your goals.

6. *Mind Your Mind*

Control your thoughts and regulate them. Discard the negatives and focus on the positives. Mistakes happen. People blunder. But that doesn't mean that you are incapable or unworthy. Treat them only as a learning experience.

7. *Get a New Hobby*

Find something that interests you and give it a shot. If you are good at it, engage in that activity at least once a week. If you find you enjoy cooking, cook yourself a good meal and enjoy it. If you like painting, make sure you admire your handiwork. Go a little beyond each week, and appreciate yourself with each step you take. For example, if you choose cooking, try a new, harder recipe of a dish you like and pat yourself on the back for the work you put in, even if it doesn't turn out very well. Keep at it until you get it right and celebrate when you do. These small things matter a lot in building your self-confidence. If you can learn a new recipe, you can do anything right!

8. *Face Your Fear*

> *"Inaction breeds doubt and fear. Action breeds confidence and courage. If you want to conquer fear, do not sit home and think about it. Go out and get busy."*
>
> —DALE CARNEGIE

It's time to face your fear. Reflect on how well you have been doing by looking at your list of achievements. Now, do something that you have been putting off for a while. It can be anything—like, say, getting your tooth removed. But make sure you do it. This will prove to you that you can do it.

9. Bid Adieu to Your Comfort Zone

> *"I quit being afraid when my first venture failed and the sky didn't fall down."*
> —ALLEN H. NEUHARTH

Once you face your fears, you will be able to see a surge in your confidence levels. However, that's not enough. Until now, you have only been setting yourself achievable goals. You have not stepped out of your comfort zone. You are doing only what you think you are capable of doing. How will you know what you really are capable of?

Stretch yourself and take a risk. Failure is not going to kill you. Set a goal out of your comfort zone and try with all your might to achieve it. When you do achieve it, make sure you add it to your list of achievements!

10. Dress Sharp, Stand Tall, and Smile

> *"Never bend your head. Always hold it high. Look the world straight in the face."*
> —HELEN KELLER

This might seem trifling, but your body language and your personal appearance have a great effect on your confidence. When you dress your best, you naturally carry yourself with confidence. Grooming yourself, dressing nicely, and holding your head high enhance your self-image and hence your self-confidence and portray it to others. When others appreciate you for your appearance and poise, you become more confident about yourself. When you smile often, you feel great about yourself. It helps you be kinder to others. Though small, it can have a large chain reaction.

People who lack confidence indulge constantly in comparing themselves to other people. This only leads to discouragement. Avoid the perfectionist attitude. It will bring you no good. Remember that there will always be people richer, smarter, and more competent. But the important thing is that they are not you. You have the power over yourself but not over others. If you apply yourself, you can enhance your situation and succeed. Don't let anyone tell you that you cannot succeed, including yourself.

WATCH OUT FOR OVERCONFIDENCE!

Too much of anything is good for nothing. It's possible to be too self-confident. That's what is called overconfidence. Malcolm Muggeridge, English journalist, author, and satirist, says:

> *"Never forget that only dead fish swim with the stream."*

Overconfidence is looking at a situation with a greater certainty of success than the situation warrants. It is the exaggerated belief in one's own abilities. Overconfidence is what leads to arrogance. All of us have come across such arrogant people who refuse to agree that they are wrong.

Overconfidence leads
to arrogance.

Suppose you were going on a hiking and camping trip with four of your colleagues. One of your colleagues, let's call him Mark, thinks he has a great sense of direction. He boasts to the rest of you, "Blindfold me and leave me in the middle of anywhere; I will find the way back in no time." He takes the initiative to lead you all to your camping site, a river. Thinking he really does have a good sense of direction, you decide to follow him. When one of your other colleagues offers Mark a map, he declines, saying something like, "I don't need a map; I wrote the map!"

Now you start feeling a little bit uneasy. However, you push it aside, thinking it will be fine and follow Mark. According to the Internet, it should have taken you just under three hours to reach your destination. But you have been walking for over five hours and still there's no sign of a water body. You are obviously lost! Just when you check your phone for reception for the umpteenth time and find none, you see a local man walking in the opposite direction. One of your friends approaches him for directions, but Mark stops your friend and pulls him back saying that he will figure out the way out of there and that there's no fun in adventure if you ask for directions.

You decide it's time you put your foot down. You stop the local man and ask for directions, which he gladly gives. You lead the group to the camping site and have a great time.

Overconfidence is an exaggerated belief in one's own abilities.

Why did Mark refuse to accept help or admit that he was lost? It's because he was overconfident in his abilities and asking for directions would only mean that he was wrong, which would hurt his pride.

Overconfidence is said to have potentially catastrophic implications. Mark's story was just a small example of what overconfidence can lead to. Your overconfidence could even cost you your job. If you are overconfident when you are driving a bike or a car, it could even result in the loss of lives.

FIVE TIPS TO BATTLE OVERCONFIDENCE

Overconfidence happens to everyone. It prevents us from learning more and becoming truly competent. But how do you check your overconfidence? Here are a few strategies to control your confidence:

1. Be honest with yourself. Recognize your limits and accept them. You can work on them but you cannot oversee them.

2. Stop comparing yourself with others. When you compare, you might think you are inferior to others, but you might also think less of others' abilities and skills. This feeling of superiority would make you feel more sure of yourself than you actually merit.

3. Value criticism, especially constructive criticism from people you trust. No one is perfect. Criticism is just an opportunity to work on your shortcomings. Don't miss that.

4. Think before you commit to anything. Overconfidence might lead you to commit to more than what you can. Be realistic and weigh your resources before you promise anything.

5. Don't overstretch yourself. Take risks, but take calculated risks that are worthy of your time and resources.

Keep in my mind that you are a unique individual with your own set of skills, abilities, and limits. Be confident of yourself but also develop a sense of modesty. This would allow you to keep overconfidence in check.

CHAPTER REWIND

- Confidence leads to determination, the harbinger of success.

- Self-confident people have a higher probability of making it big than people who doubt their own abilities.

- Your self-confidence leaves a deep impact on those around you.

- To improve your self-confidence, you have to work on your self-esteem and self-efficacy.

- Remember the journey from confidence to overconfidence is a short and a slippery one. Overconfidence prevents us from learning more and becoming truly competent. Keep it under control at all times.

Chapter 5

UNWAVERING FAITH

"The only thing that stands between a man and what he wants from life is often merely the will to try it and the faith to believe that it is possible."
—RICHARD M. DEVOS

STEPHEN KING AND *CARRIE*

Stephen King's books are famous the world over. He has published 50 novels, 5 non-fiction books, and nearly 200 short stories. His books have sold over 350 million copies, and many of them have been adapted as feature films, television movies, and comics. His first break and one of his most notable works was *Carrie*.

Stephen King started writing *Carrie* when his family was living in a trailer. At first, he threw away the initial few pages he had written. But his wife, Tabitha, fished out the pages from the garbage and motivated him to continue writing it. So, did the first publisher to whom he sent the book simply fall in love with the book and agree to publish it? No. Nor did the second one or 28 other publishers. He received around 30 rejections before it was accepted!

With his wife's support, King simply continued sending his manuscript to other publishers until it was accepted. *Carrie* became so famous that it sold over 1 million copies in the first year alone and was adapted as three feature films, a Broadway musical, and a television movie!

One of the publishers who had rejected Carrie had said, "We are not interested in science fiction, which deals with negative utopias. They do not sell." *Carrie* broke several records and went on to become a classic in the genre of horror.

FAITH WATERS IDEAS TO REALITY

Ideas—that's where everything starts. There are hundreds and thousands of different businesses and services today. Great ideas become great inventions, save lives, and make life easier. But they all arise from the same point—a small thought in someone's mind. These seeds of thoughts become the seeds for success. They are crucial, not only in your professional life, but also in your personal life. If your family is facing a problem, a good idea can help you turn your situation around. An idea can give your career a boost; save your marriage; help you start your own business; or bring you fame, power, and money. Even this book was an idea first. There are no failed ideas, just failed execution, as Seth Godin said:

"There isn't a shortage of ideas. There's a shortage of execution."

You create your goals based on your ideas, which when achieved become success. Ideas fire passion, instill confidence, and bring about determination, which takes you to your destination. But what makes an idea do all this? Yes, faith. Solid, unwavering faith in your ideas brings about the confidence to go through the entire process of execution. If we don't believe in our ideas, then they will be mere thoughts floating in our minds, just like a million others.

In the last chapter, we saw how crucial confidence in our abilities is for our success. Faith in our ideas is an extension of that. Self-confidence engenders creativity, creativity fosters ideas, and faith transforms the ideas into reality. If you have an idea, you have to be your biggest cheerleader. If you reject it before even considering it as a possibility, how would you know if you it was a good idea or a bad idea?

Faith drives motivation.

Stephen King, for instance, kept on trying because he believed in his idea. People may mock your ideas, friends and/or family may discourage you, but if you stop believing in your ideas, then they can never see the daylight. Don't overthink your idea. Nurture it. Protect it from external criticism or influence. The more you believe in your idea, the more real it becomes. As your idea becomes clearer, it matures, enhancing your enthusiasm and faith in it.

The initial enthusiasm and belief in your idea is unadulterated. It feels like magic. It happens before you have analyzed your idea. Before you line up the reasons why it might or might not work. This is the feeling that makes it happen. This feeling of pure belief lets you visualize your idea. If you retain this belief at every stage of execution, your ideas can undergo the transformation and your visualization can become a reality.

> *"Ideas can be life-changing. Sometimes all you need to open the door is just one more good idea."*
>
> —JIM ROHN

FAITH EQUALS MOTIVATION

Your faith in your idea and confidence in yourself become your motivation. Faith and needs are what drive motivation. When people have needs, it motivates them to do something to fulfil them. When people believe in something, it pushes them to make it true. For instance, you have the need to earn enough money to keep your family hale and happy. That motivates you to find a way to earn money— you either get a job or start your business. You believe that what you have earned will be enough for the month. This drives you to work harder to make your earnings enough. It could be summed up as a formula:

MOTIVATION = FAITH X NEED

If either the need or the faith is absent, there is no motivation. But such as it is, people always have needs. Our needs never end. If a person is financially constrained, he yearns to attain financial independence. But once he attains that, his needs don't stop there. They multiply. Now, he might need a family. When he finds his life partner and begins a family, his needs multiply again. He might now need a higher payroll to satisfy the needs of his family.

As you keep fulfilling your needs, they keep increasing exponentially, especially with the advancement in technology, which keeps inventing new things to make your life better. Before, you could do with a landline phone at home. When mobile phones were introduced, you needed one for whatever reason. Now, it's the era of the smartphones. It's not just desire, and you don't simply want a smartphone, you need one. Life today is so dependent on technology that if you don't keep pace with it, you are rudely left behind. This is why it's so difficult to find a satisfied person these days.

So, we have established that one of the factors of motivation is perpetually present. You can't simply take it out of the equation. But why do you often find so many unmotivated people? It's because of the absence of faith in themselves or in their ideas.

Imagine you have a problem at work. The project you are working on is stuck. You are unable to move forward or backward; you are simply stuck in one place. You surely have faced this at least once. You brainstorm with your friend at work and come up with a way to solve your problem. So, your need is to move your project in some direction, hopefully toward a favorable direction. You have also found a possible solution to fulfill your need. But before you even try it, you think it will not work. You don't have the faith that it will benefit you or help you in any way. Will you be motivated, then, to try the solution? On the other hand, imagine if you even have the slightest notion that your idea just might click; won't you be motivated to try it, at least once?

THERE IS NEVER TOO MUCH FAITH

Every idea is a potential solution to a persisting problem. However ridiculous it may sound, entertain an idea just long enough to see what becomes of it. Sometimes, you might reject an idea just because you don't have the resources or something is beyond your understanding. You won't always have the knowledge it requires. But that comes on the execution side, after you decide to put your plan into action.

When a potential solution occurs to you, the question you must ask before simply rejecting it is, "If I learn what is necessary to execute the idea, will it be successful?" Then the process of learning, developing skills, and gathering resources becomes the first stage of execution.

Being passionate enough and believing in your ideas is important for you to commit to the learning process. You might not know everything yet, but if you believe in your idea you will try it, and unless you try it, you cannot come up with better solutions. Remember Edison's first thousand attempts to devise the first practical incandescent light. If he hadn't gone through all one thousand and given up at some point, someone else may have taken it from there. Don't start an idea by thinking it isn't good enough. If you are ready to do what it takes, you might be able to transform the idea.

Don't start an idea by thinking it isn't good enough. You cannot be guided by the fear of rejection and fear of failure.

FAITH EXPELS FEAR

You cannot be guided by the fear of rejection and fear of failure. But when fear dominates in your mind, how can you overcome it? By believing in your ideas. It is your faith that motivates you to work for it and to keep going. Only if you believe it will work will you be able to develop the skills necessary for achieving what you visualize.

"Believe it is possible to solve your problem. Tremendous things happen to the believer. So believe the answer will come. It will."

—NORMAN VINCENT PEALE

Do you know of FedEx? Of course you do. Everybody knows FedEx. But did you know FedEx, previously called Federal Express, was the first overnight express delivery company in the world? You probably knew that too. The founder of FedEx, Frederick Smith, came up with the idea of overnight delivery for a term paper in college. Do you know what grade he received for it? C! What if Smith had given up after the first attempt, thinking maybe it wasn't meant to be? The world would still have got its overnight express delivery company, only Smith would not have been its founder, chairman, president, and CEO.

If you think it doesn't matter, ask people who didn't lose anything; ask countless others who had actually given up and watched their ideas transformed into inventions, revolutions, and solutions by others. You might have heard some people say that some brilliant product or service was their idea. While some of this may be fallacy, some turn out to be true.

To have complete faith does not mean that you blindly believe in anything. It means that you proceed with each step, right from the stage when your ideas are simply thoughts, by thinking, "Let's say that it works—what next?" or "If I learn how to do that, what next?" When you do this, you will be able to analyze your idea without any prejudice and evaluate its merit.

If you think you might face some problem or challenge when you execute it, don't drop it altogether but think how you should approach the problem and overcome it. This will give birth to another idea and another, until it becomes a foolproof solution to your problem at the office, at home, or perhaps your business's USP. Unless you believe in your solution, your friends, family, colleagues, or customers will not.

GET RID OF THE DANCING MONKEYS

Sometimes, people cannot stop thinking of the negative side of anything. Sometimes, even if we are confident and believe in our ideas, other people point us to the negative side and we are forced to see it. This discourages us from defending our own ideas. Being discouraged is easy. However, all it takes is determination to get your faith back. What's important to remember is that disbelief is not created at birth. Disbelief is put into us as we grow up. Your mind doesn't come up with sceptic thoughts. Someone says something at some point of your life; they put it in your mind. Your mind just picks it up and fixates on it.

The notions that you are too thin, too tall, or too clumsy are not yours but are put into you, most likely by your parents, siblings, or friends. Some people consider themselves unlucky—that whatever idea they come up with is bound to fail. When you were a baby, your brain wasn't filled with such notions. You think so now because someone put that notion in you with or without your knowledge. The more you think about such notions, the more they manifest.

Imagine you are going to a doctor for a sore throat and he prescribes you some pills. But right before you leave, the doctor says, "Remember, the pills will only work if you don't think about the dancing monkeys while you have it." Now, such is the power of the human mind that every time you take your pill, you will end up seeing those dancing monkeys, irrespective of how hard you try not to think about them.

Remember, disbelief is not created at birth. Disbelief is put into us as we grow up.

For some people, negative thinking is the default setting. To become positive, your brain needs some amount of programming. Say you have an empty piece of land. What happens if you don't do anything? What grows? Yes, weeds. You don't have to tend to weeds or nurture them. They just grow. Similarly, if you don't do anything about it, pessimism flourishes. You have to program your brain to be positive and protect it from becoming negative again by choosing the right company of people, reading the right books, and cultivating the right habits. As George Bernard Shaw said:

> *"Never wrestle with a pig. You both get dirty and the pig likes it."*

STOP ANALYZING AND START ACTING

Sometimes, it is best to stop analyzing and start acting. The problem with analyzing too much is that there is a risk the problem will no longer be the same problem after you have finished with it. Either it will have magnified, or it will have become obsolete. Either way, you are only wasting time by analyzing.

Let's say a man is waiting at an airport lounge. He has some time and he is bored. He looks around and sees a fortune-telling machine. Curiosity gets the better of him and, thinking he has to kill time anyhow, he goes ahead and inserts a coin. The multicolored lights on the machine go on and off for a few seconds and then the machine spits out a small card. The card reads: "Your name is Mohammed, you weigh 75 kilograms, and you are on the 20:30 flight to New York."

The man is now completely astounded. Even though he is a non-believer, he cannot fathom how the machine could know his name and destination. He thinks that maybe someone is playing a trick on him. Excited to solve this mystery, he goes away, shaves his moustache, wears a hat and shades, and comes back. He inserts a coin and the machine spits out another card, which reads: "Your name is still Mohammed, you still weigh 75 kilograms, and you are on the 20:30 flight to New York."

The man just cannot believe this. He takes it as a challenge to uncover the mystery. This time, he changes his t-shirt, shaves his head, comes back to the machine, and inserts another coin. The card now reads: "Your name is still Mohammed, you still weigh 75 kilograms, but you've just missed your 20:30 flight to New York!"

Ideas become stale if you don't act upon them.

Are you waiting for the machine's secret? Well, that is exactly the point. The story here is not to be analyzed, but to be acted upon. We cannot possibly analyze everything we come across. Sometimes, we need to just go ahead and act. Otherwise, while we are analyzing, our opportunity may pass.

This is the case with ideas too. That doesn't mean you shouldn't analyze your ideas at all. By all means, go ahead— analyze them. But just don't overdo it. If you feel you need some push to get you started, here are some ways to help you roll your sleeves up and start doing something about your ideas.

1. *Portray It Well*

Let's say you are sharing an idea with your friend. How you put it also matters. Suppose you put a self-deprecating question at the end, like, "It's stupid, isn't it?" or "Will it work, or am I just crazy?" What you are actually doing here is that even before your friend forms an opinion of your idea, you are forming it for her. You are putting the dancing monkeys in her mind. How is your friend supposed to think of the true merit of the idea with the monkeys dancing before her eyes?

Imagine you are putting your idea forward to Warren Buffet, who is considering investing in your business. Would he even evaluate your idea if you portrayed it in such a manner? Probably in a perfect world! You are putting your friend in the same predicament by adding the self-deprecating question at the end.

Your level of enthusiasm also has a great effect on your friend, who is listening to your ideas. In fact, it's more important than your idea itself because she catches your enthusiasm before you even begin. If you are indifferent or dispassionate, you are only making it harder for her to take you seriously.

2. *Never Say "Later"*

Some people say that an idea matures when you put it to rest and come back to it later. But there's also a chance that you might forget to go back or you might lose your enthusiasm. Sometimes, you might even forget the idea itself! Ravi, a fresh graduate, approached his uncle Ram, a successful entrepreneur, one day and said that he had a great idea for a fiction novel. After he told Ram the seed of the story, he proceeded to say how it might be boring and how no one would read it if he wrote it.

Ram, a man of few words simply told him, "Write the book first. Then we will decide if it's interesting or not." There's no way you will know if it's a good idea or a bad idea unless you do it. And there will always be people who claim it will not work. You are only procrastinating your moment. Do it and find out for yourself if your idea is good or bad.

3. *Tell Someone*

When you tell someone that you are going to do something, you are making a commitment. If you don't fulfil your commitment, you are going to look bad in front of that person. This will then motivate you to work on executing your idea. This will also show that you do have faith in your idea and that you can make it work if you wanted to.

When you make a commitment, it also shows that you have made a decision. You are not going to sit with your idea; you are going to do something about it. Sometimes, all it takes for you to start working is for you to accept that you will be doing it no matter what. Your indecision will only infect your faith and distort it.

Your commitment will therefore overthrow the disbelief and the negativity and declare your faith and decision. This will let you move forward. If your faith seems to waver at any point during execution, make a decision again and again, and you will keep moving forward.

4. Think "Next"

"What's the next step that I can take immediately?" is the most crucial question of all. This will stop all the questioning, doubting, and excuses that you are likely to make to not execute your idea.

Suppose you are a songwriter and you have an idea for a song. Sit and write it. Nobody is going to question you or mock you about your idea. What could they say? "Have you gone crazy? Why are you writing a song?" This is because you are doing something about your idea.

If you don't do anything about your idea, then it's just going to sit in your brain. Your brain then comes up with the biggest fears or excuses why you shouldn't do it. Don't overthink it, just start with the first step. That's how you show that you have faith in your ideas.

It doesn't have to be a huge step. It can be anything as small as starting to read about what you don't know or chalking out a plan for execution. Once you take the first step, your enthusiasm and determination should help you move it forward.

So, what's your next step going to be?

CHAPTER REWIND
CHAPTER REWIND

- An idea can give your career a boost; save your marriage; help you start your own business; or bring you fame, power, and money.

- You create your goals based on your ideas, which when achieved become success.

- You need to believe in your ideas to overcome the fear of rejection.

- Complete faith does not mean that you blindly believe in anything. Proceed step by step, analyze your idea without any prejudice, and evaluate its merit.

- You cannot possibly analyze everything you come across. Sometimes you need to just go ahead and act.

Chapter 6

BALANCING DETERMINATION AND PASSION

"When I have finally decided that a result is worth getting, I go ahead and make trial after trial until it comes."
—THOMAS ALVA EDISON

"You can have anything you want if you want it desperately enough. You must want it with an exuberance that erupts through the skin and joins the energy that created the world."
—SHEILA GRAHAM

TWO THOUSAND PER DAY

Young Michael Jordan, who went on to become the world-famous basketball champion, was told by his high school basketball coach that he was not good enough, that he would never make the team! What did he do? He took it to his heart. He promised himself that that would never happen to him again. He pushed himself to improve his abilities and worked harder than ever. Every day after he returned from school, he would practice shots on the nets. Not ten or twenty, but only after making two thousand successful shots would he be satisfied. Two thousand baskets every single day! The whole world knows now that his tenacity paid off. In 1981, he received a basketball scholarship, and in 1984 he entered the NBA draft, where the Chicago Bulls picked him. From there, there was no looking back for Michael Jordan.

AGAIN AND AGAIN, AND YET AGAIN UNTIL SUCCESS

Michael's story explains determination. This ability to strive for something, to constantly push ourselves to do our best no matter how difficult the goal seems, is determination. It is one of the most important predictors of success. It has a great impact on our lives.

Sachin Tendulkar, who is considered the god of cricket in India, did not achieve that status overnight. World tennis champion Rafael Nadal had to strive hard to come to this position. Muhammad Ali, the legendary boxer who earned the name "The People's Champion," toiled day and night before he earned it.

Even though this trait is more evident in the field of sports, determination is almost always the precursor of success in any field. You are probably more familiar with the story of how Thomas Alva Edison invented the first commercially practical incandescent light bulb. Before arriving at the formula for the light bulb as we know it, Edison made one thousand attempts. But when asked about it, Edison simply said:

"I have not failed a thousand times. I have not failed once. I have succeeded in proving that those one thousand ways will not work. When I have eliminated the ways that will not work, I will find the way that will work."

Forming goals is easy. But only a few people have what it takes to finish something they started. Have you heard the story of Karoly Takacs, who was the first shooter to win two gold medals in the Olympic rapid-fire pistol event? That's not just it. Takacs won the first medal using his right hand and the second using his left hand after he lost his right hand in a grenade accident! When Takacs lost his right hand, he did not get dejected. He simply got a left-handed pistol, practiced harder, went back, and won his medal.

You don't have to push yourself to achieve what you cannot. Everyone has his/her own abilities. Knowing your true potential and playing to your strengths is very important. With your abilities, you can probably achieve your friend's goals easily. Someone else may find your goals achievable. It's all about knowing how much you can do and working hard to make sure that you do not fall short on your potential.

ENTRY TICKET OR CHAMPIONSHIP?

Determination is perhaps the most overlooked quality, one that can take you not just to the path of success but right to the destination. As we saw before, determination is what determines whether you will succeed or not. What about talent, then?

It is a popular notion that talent or intelligence is the sole requirement to succeed. "My boy is very talented; he will go places." This is what we normally hear. This is what we believe. But unfortunately, your talent or intelligence alone will not take you to success. Sure, it's important. It does not mean that talent is not required, only that talent is overrated. There are millions of talented artists in the world. But not all of them turn into Picassos or Van Goghs or Monets. There are millions of people with great ideas. But not all of them become Henry Ford or Steven Spielberg.

Determination is the most overlooked quality.

Talent or intelligence is simply like the eligibility criteria for securing a place at a university. It's the entry ticket—a qualification you must possess to succeed.

Suppose you want to become fit. The first thing you have to do is sign up at a health club. But just because you sign up, does it mean you will become fit? You have to work hard for it. Similarly, possessing talent is important. But if you don't put it to use, you cannot hope to get much out of it. Talent, simply put, is not the deciding factor.

Then why is talent overrated when compared to determination? Because talent provides an excuse to the others, the spectators, to be lazy. Also because, when someone combines determination and talent, determination starts looking like talent after a while.

Determination is almost always the precursor of success in any field.

There's a great story about Sachin Tendulkar. Everyone knows what a talented cricket player he is. Some years ago, before a test match between India and Australia, the teams played a warm up game. During the warm up match, Sachin noticed that Shane Warne, the legendary Australian bowler, did not go around the wicket even once when he bowled to him. He thought that Warne was probably saving that for the test match. He couldn't rest. He started practicing that particular kind of ball every day before the test match until he got it. In the test, when Warne bowled that particular ball to Sachin, the whole world went "wow" at the expertise with which he tackled the spinning deliveries. If Sachin had been confident about his talent and not bothered to practice, he may not have got that result.

BE THE SUN, NOT A SHOOTING STAR

There are plenty of people who possess the talent but not the determination and fade like shooting stars. You can see such people mainly in the field of sports because of the fame and publicity it gets. How many sportspersons have you noticed perform amazingly in a couple of matches or events and vanish without a trace after that? What differentiates such shooting stars from the stars that stay fixed in the minds of fans long after their tenure is their tenacity. It's the sheer determination to just not give up until you have achieved your true potential that brings you closer to success.

Whether you want to achieve something with your talent (for everyone has some kind of talent) or you want to let it rot is your choice. One of the main things that helps you make the right choice is to create your goals and always keep an eye on the prize. This lets you become more focused and prioritizes your life so that you can give way for determination to save the day.

CAN DETERMINATION BE CULTIVATED?

We have defined determination as the ability to not back out and push yourself to achieve your dreams. If determination is your inner drive, can you cultivate determination? Absolutely! Is it unbelievable? Let's analyze the reason behind this by dissecting the components of determination.

What is determination made of? There are three main attributes of determination—willpower, discipline, and ambition.

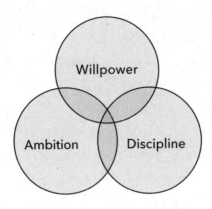

THE THREE COMPONENTS OF DETERMINATION

1. *Willpower*

Willpower is the strength to carry out what you wish—your dreams, plans, or decisions. This is the simplest form of determination. If you are strong-willed, you will have the power to keep going until you achieve what you wanted. But willpower is something that is inborn. It's common in families where one sibling is much more strong-willed than the other. Circumstances can make slight impacts, but nature plays the higher hand compared to nurture when it comes to willpower. Bad situations can break the willpower of a strong-willed person, but it's difficult to turn a weak-willed person into a strong-willed person.

2. *Discipline*

Just having strong willpower is not enough. You have to have strict work ethic and discipline to achieve what you want. People who are strong-willed but lack discipline are not determined, but self-indulgent. There has to be a balance between discipline and willpower. The more strong-willed you are, the more disciplined you need to be. Why is this?

When you have the will to do what you want to do, the temptations around you increase. If you are just strong-willed but not disciplined, chances are you give in to the temptations and stray away from your goals. Discipline lets you focus your willpower on your ultimate goals and prevents you from going away from your target.

Fortunately, discipline is something that you can cultivate. Discipline is the result of removing your temptations and setting out to follow your plan. Discipline comes with practice and gradually becomes a habit. If you set aside one hour of your day to read about your field, then switch off the stupid box, sit down, and do it. If you find you can get extra hours with effective time management, do it. Be dedicated in what you want to achieve and think only about that.

3. Ambition

Ambition is what drives you to be determined. It is the strong desire to achieve something. Ambitiousness can be both natural and inspired. You need not be born ambitious. Everyone has the ability to develop a strong drive. Circumstances play a major role. If you are surrounded by ambitious people, you get inspired and encouraged by them and become ambitious yourself.

If you aren't naturally driven, books play a significant role in cultivating ambition. The more you read, the more you know. The more you know, the more you would like to do something with what you know. This becomes a constant motivation and feeds your willpower to achieve your goals. Reading a lot of inspirational books, therefore, can help you develop ambition. Learning from your role model or people who inspire you also gives you the drive to follow suit. Let's add one more formula in this book:

DETERMINATION = WILLPOWER X DISCIPLINE X AMBITION

Two out of three components of determination can be developed. So, what do you think? Can you not develop determination?

PASSION—THE KEY TO LIVING A MEANINGFUL LIFE

James M. Barrie, Scottish dramatist and novelist who created Peter Pan, said:

> *"Nothing is really work unless you would rather be doing something else."*

Talent and determination are not the only factors in success. How much you enjoy your work is also important. If you really love what you do, you don't need to develop the drive to work. You already have it.

There was an article in *Fortune* magazine about James Cramer, the former hedge fund manager and best-selling author. Cramer would wake up at 4:00 a.m. every day so that he could read five different newspapers to get a head start. He would then work the whole day and go back for a mere three hours of sleep. Why did he work so hard? Did he need money that badly? No, not really. Did he want to be rich? Not possible; he was already wealthy. There is a simple reason for it. He worked so hard because he loved his work!

Perhaps he was a little extreme. However, the important thing is when you wake up every morning, you should be happy to go to work.

Passion for your work makes your life meaningful.

You should work not because you have to, but because you enjoy working. Instead, if you wake up feeling depressed about having to get ready and drag yourself to work, you would be living a rather meaningless life. You may retort saying that not many of us like going to work. That's saying a lot about the quality of life we are leading, don't you think?

Why do you think this generation is changing jobs more than ever? It's the restlessness and the frustration of doing what they don't like. People are more motivated by the money they can earn. They choose jobs that have a higher payroll without considering if they would enjoy their work. Passion for your work should be one of the main criteria when it comes to your career.

Let's say you hate finance. How many years can you stay in a job as a finance manager? One? Two? Whole life?

If you were unfortunate to have to stay in your job for most of your life, how much effort would you put in your job? Would you put your heart into every challenge you face at work? Or would you rather earn your salary by just showing up and warming your seat at work?

Motivational speaker, author, and entrepreneur Steve Pavlina once said:

> *"Hard work is painful when life is devoid of purpose. But when you live for something greater than yourself and the gratification of your own ego, then hard work becomes a labor of love."*

Instead, imagine that you love finance management. You would voluntarily work harder, longer, and better. It's human nature to seek and prolong what we enjoy. This would only make you more productive. Ultimately, you would keep moving higher and higher up in your organization. You wouldn't feel that your boss is forcing work upon you. You would be ready to do above and beyond what's expected of you.

You would put in your maximum efforts. You would love the challenges even more because challenges help you learn new things about finance and let you come up with new ideas. Challenges also allow you to compete with yourself. Happiness reaches a new level when you discover that you can beat your own records! This happiness in your career would reflect in your personal life, in turn making your family happy.

Work not because you have to, but because you enjoy working.

A lifetime doing what you enjoy is so much more meaningful and productive than a lifetime doing something that you hate. Passion does not necessarily mean doing what others consider as cool, artistic things. People often jump to this conclusion. Being the lead guitarist of a band is definitely considered cool. But imagine you hate playing the guitar, even though you can play moderately well. If you become a lead guitarist just to earn money and fame, you would consider your life dull. On the other hand, what others may find dull, you may enjoy.

We often come across people who complain that their life is monotonous. People have the notion that if they did what they enjoyed, their life would not feel like a routine. This is wrong, because that's how life is—routine. If your routine were disturbed every day, you would feel constantly irritated. We may think that we hate routine, but our body constantly finds patterns and organizes them to create a routine. Our body functions at its optimum level only if everything occurs according to our inner clock. Similarly, if our mind cannot find a pattern in what we do, we become frustrated.

Suppose you are a person who does not like going out much. But because your family insists, you plan a long trip.

At first, you would probably enjoy it immensely. Slowly, however, you would lose all the enthusiasm and excitement. You would be itching to come back home because that's what your routine is. If, on the other hand, you were an outgoing person, you would hate to stay at home for a long time. Routine is different to each person, but when your routine is disturbed, you feel restless.

Even when you pursue a career in what you think is your passion, you will find that your job involves routine things to do. Don't give up your career thinking that you are at the wrong place just because you have to do similar things each day.

PASSION—FOLLOWING VS. CULTIVATING

A quote by American physician and NASA astronaut Mae Jemison goes thus:

> *"It's your place in the world; it's your life. Go on and do all you can with it, and make it the life you want to live."*

What does cultivating your passion mean? Let me share the story of David with you. When David was in middle school, he read an article called "Follow Your Passion" on the Internet one day. A successful musician, who had found his love for music at a very young age, had written the article. David was fascinated by the idea of finding his true passion and making a career in it. Young David discussed this with his parents and asked if it were true. His parents said that this was indeed true and encouraged him to find what he liked doing the best.

Since then, David promised himself that by the time he graduated from high school, he would have found his passion. He tried many things and enrolled himself in science, math, and literature clubs and painting and music classes. He had the idea that when he found his passion, he would know it, like it would ring some sort of bell in him. No bells rang.

David had graduated high school but he couldn't put a finger on what he liked the best. He had narrowed it down to two, based on what he was good at—math and painting, but neither invoked joy in him, as was supposed to happen according to the stories he had read. Moreover, the two were so different that he didn't know which he should choose. He was tormented by the fear of choosing the wrong field and having to be stuck with it his entire life. His parents were depressed by his inability to make a decision. They took the matter in their hands. Dejected, but having no other option, David studied math as his major in college.

He was good at math, but he failed to see it. He was constantly frustrated, thinking that maybe he wasn't meant to be there. Perhaps he was supposed to be a musician and he missed out on it. When he couldn't take it anymore, he quit his college and joined music school. Did he find his passion in music? Unfortunately, no. He was utterly disappointed in himself and in life, and spent his life in regret and guilt.

What does David's story tell us? That following our passion is wrong? No. This tells us that passion and excitement are two different things and that passion, as portrayed by the media, is delusional.

Passion and excitement are two different things.

Only a few are lucky, because they have a clear passion. Perhaps such people have always wanted to be scientists, doctors, pianists, or writers. To them, the advice of following their passion makes sense. However, this puts a huge pressure on the rest of us. We develop the idea that if we are not careful, we might miss our true calling. We are not free of this thought even after we make a decision. Every time we face a difficult challenge or a setback and the going gets tough, the obnoxious, unanswerable question torments us, "Am I doing what I'm meant to be doing?" This leads to anxiety, depression, and chronic job-hopping.

If you are among the lucky few, then you know what to do. But what should the rest of us do? We should cultivate passion in what we do. The anxiety and depression is only a result of the notion you have. Shake it off. What makes you truly enjoy your work is based on several factors—your competency, your thoughts on how valuable you are to your organization, and autonomy. Several years of studies back this up.

Cal Newport, computer scientist and faculty at Georgetown University, debunked the belief that "follow your passion" is good advice in his book, *So Good They Can't Ignore You.* There is little evidence to suggest that people have preexisting passions. There is no perfect career option waiting to be discovered by you. He says that instead of following their passion based on some romanticized notion, people should cultivate passion in what they do. This gives you flexibility, because when you are ready to cultivate passion in what you do, you have a number of jobs that you can transform to be your passion.

Instead of asking yourself, "What is my passion?" you should ask, "How can I develop passion in my work?"

BE DETERMINED AND MAKE PASSION FOLLOW YOU

Often we find that people get excited about an idea, but after trying it only a few times they lose their drive to execute their idea. Why does this happen? Because people have a mistaken definition for passion. Excitement about a particular idea produces a sensation completely different from what true passion, which drives people to make their careers successful, creates. What is true passion, then?

True passion arises after you toil hard and put in extra effort to develop the skills required for your field and become the best in what you do. Passion lets you leverage your value to gain autonomy and respect and to control your professional career.

True passion comes after you become good at what you do.

This means that you can transform your dull professional life into a career full of value. You can control what you achieve in your career. You need not follow passion; passion will follow you. Isn't that wonderful? Here are some strategies to help you go about that.

1. *Be flexible, not specific.*

The advantage of knowing the true meaning of passion is that you don't have to wait and daydream until you find your true calling. You have a host of different jobs in which you can cultivate your passion. When you are looking at a new job, ask, "Will this job be interesting if I become good at it?" Don't think about what you will be doing specifically, as your job specifications will change as you progress in your career. Instead, think of what environment your job will provide you and whether it will be conducive for you to become good at the job. Choose a position based on this.

2. *Focus on what you can offer your job.*

Do not see what your job can offer you. See what you can offer for your job. Compare this with what is expected from your position. Bridge the gap by developing the necessary skills. When you are starting a new job, don't think whether you like the job. Think how you can better yourself.

3. *Become competent; autonomy will follow.*

No one ever said that success comes without hard work. No pain, no gain. Be determined to become good at your job. When you become competent at what you do, you become valuable to your organization. The more valuable you are, the more satisfaction you get out of your job. Besides, the feeling of being good at your work itself will give you satisfaction. Anyone can testify to this.

Also, the more value you offer to your organization, the more freedom you will be given to choose what you do and how you do it. Being autonomous also provides great satisfaction.

4. *Use your value to your advantage.*

Don't stop when you have become competent and valuable to your organization. Leverage your value to reach your dream lifestyle. If you want to be in the thick of things, then leverage your value to take charge of a new department in your organization. If you crave for being the man behind the scenes, then find a suitable role accordingly.

But if you jump into your dream lifestyle without gaining value, it will only lead to failure. For example, moving to a reclusive place to write books is a great plan. But if you haven't put in the effort to become a good writer, it's not sustainable. On the other hand, there are people who never leverage the value they have earned. Work hard with determination to become skilled, but also recognize your value and use it after you become skilled. Otherwise, there's no room for progress.

Cultivating determination and using it to cultivate passion in what you do will take you toward a successful career and a fulfilling life.

CHAPTER REWIND
CHAPTER REWIND

- Determination is the ability to strive for something, to constantly push yourself to do your best.

- It's all about knowing how much you can do and working hard to make sure you do not fall short on your potential.

- While talent is overrated, determination is underrated. Talent doesn't stand a chance without determination.

- Determination can be cultivated. Discipline, willpower, and ambition build determination.

- A lifetime doing what you enjoy is much more meaningful and productive than a lifetime doing something that you hate.

- Passion is not all euphoria. Passion too has mundane and routine activities.

- Instead of following passion based on romanticized notions, cultivate passion in what you do.

Chapter 7

BUILDING THE WEB OF RELATIONSHIPS

"Your outlook upon life, your estimate of yourself, your estimate of your value are largely colored by your environment. Your whole career will be modified, shaped, molded by your surroundings, by the character of the people with whom you come in contact every day."
—ORISON SWETT MARDEN

NANCY'S STORY

Nancy, young and resourceful, was a budding PR professional. Jason, a prospective client of her firm, had fixed a business dinner with her. Their dinner had just begun, and he was amazed to find her already on friendly terms with the waiter handling their table.

During the entire course of their dinner, she maintained a great rapport with the waiter. When the evening ended, the waiter surprised Jason by giving them a 50 percent discount on their bill, just like that! The waiter even gave Nancy his card, asking her to give him a call in case she wanted a table reserved at the last moment any time in the future.

When they walked out of the restaurant, Jason asked her if she were a regular there. That was when she told him that she had never been there before, but things like this always happened wherever she went. Although impressed, Jason was bold enough to ask her if she liked to make friends for things like this to happen. Good-natured as she was and understanding that he was just joking, she laughed saying that it was because she was friendly that people were nice to her.

After that, Jason met Nancy on several occasions and became good friends. He later found that she was great at her job. She enjoyed her work immensely, as she really liked interacting with people and making friends. She often said that it was because she could meet different people that she chose PR as her career. She was so amiable and outgoing that people who met her could not help liking her. Wherever she went, she made friends. So much so, that everyone from superiors to low-rank employees knew Nancy at every hangout she frequented!

A BLESSING NAMED RELATIONSHIP

"Do you know about stock investment? I would like to invest, but I don't know much about them."

"No, but one of my friends works for a stockbroking agency. I can introduce you to her."

"Thanks, that would be perfect!"

You must have had one such conversation with someone in your life. You might have thought that you are helping out a friend, or assisting two mutually beneficial parties to come together. But what you are actually doing is being a catalyst to relationship building through your contacts.

Humans desire friendship and positive interaction.

A decade or two ago, social networking sites might not even have existed in dreams, but now people cannot stay in touch with their friends, business associates, and sometimes even family without Facebook, Twitter, Google+, or LinkedIn. Be it getting in touch with your old buddies, finding your life partner, securing a job, or closing business deals, you can achieve everything through these networking sites.

Why do you think social networking sites have emerged to become such an integral part of our lives? It is because everyone is now aware of the significance of establishing and maintaining relationships—both in personal and professional life.

THE PEOPLE POWER

So, why are relationships important? Fundamentally, we are social creatures. Just as much as we crave food and water, we desire friendship and positive interaction. It's people who inspire us to create our goals, people who motivate us to achieve our goals, and people who encourage us in the face of difficulty. It's because we care for our family, friends, and co-workers that we work hard to overcome challenges in our life.

A solid, healthy relationship can be one of your greatest blessings, as it can provide you the strongest support you ever need. Every aspect of your life is affected by your relationships. Good relationships strengthen your mind and body and help improve your connection with others. Bad relationships, on the other hand, can drain your energy, infect your mind, and prevent you from focusing on anything else.

Each relationship is different, but they all matter. The relationship that you have with your grocery store manager is different from what you have with your boss, which in turn is different from what you have with your spouse. However, each has its own value and affects your life.

You may think that your relationship with your grocery store manager does not really affect your life in any way. You are wrong. Imagine you are on your way home after a really bad day at the office. Your kids ask you to pick something up from the grocer on your way home. At first, you are irritated at having to take a detour. But you love your kids. So, you take the detour anyway, cursing your boss.

You enter the store, pick up what you need, and walk to the checkout counter. As you approach the counter, the manager recognizes you and gives you a warm smile. He then asks about your family and your day. You tell him that you had a lousy day. He genuinely sympathizes with you and reassures you that things are bound to get better.

How great would it feel? This conversation would lift your mood and turn your awful day around. Now suppose you have a bad relationship with the grocer. He might only add to your frustration and dampen your mood. You might direct displaced anger at your spouse and kids, which might only lead to more relationship problems, but serious ones this time.

RELATIONSHIPS AT WORK THAT WORK

Strong relationships in our professional life can give the boost to our career at the right time. As Henry Ford puts it:

> *"Coming together is a beginning; keeping together is progress; working together is success."*

The well-known Aesop's fable of the four oxen and the lion brings out the moral, "United we stand, divided we fall." When people work together, great things can be accomplished.

However, relationships in your professional life are not just about teamwork. Why do companies organize offsite team-building retreats, social events, and parties? This is because better work relationships lead to a happier and more productive work environment. When you have good relationships at work, it makes your work more enjoyable. This in turn fosters innovation and creativity.

Good relationships also provide you personal space and freedom; instead of spending your time and energy on problems associated with negative relationships, you can direct them at being more committed to your work and grabbing opportunities at the right time. It would also help you implement the changes you desire in yourself and at your workplace. This will open the door to key projects and pave the way for advancement in your career and ultimately for individual growth and the growth of your organization.

However, focusing only on your professional relationships would not help you. British conservative politician, aristocrat, and writer Benjamin Disraeli rightly said:

"No success in public life can compensate for failure in the home."

When you have a healthy relationship at home, you can turn to your family for support and guidance if you face problems in your professional life. However, if you have problems in your family relationships as well, it can distract your attention and redirect your energy. You would feel drained, helpless, and lonely. This can even sabotage your career.

TAKEAWAYS OF GOOD RELATIONSHIPS

Good relationships do more than provide you emotional strength and support. They can be beneficial in many ways. Good relationships with your colleagues and superiors might work in your favor when you are being evaluated for a promotion or when you go for a change of job. Your contacts might even help you find a job. Nearly 85 percent of career openings are filled through word of mouth and personal contacts in America!

Relationships just for the sake of getting something in return will not get you anywhere.

The benefits of good relationships are not just limited to your career. Take the case of non-profit organizations and community service foundations. Only a few people join a community group or an organization because they believe in their cause. Most of them join because they have a relationship with someone who is already involved with the organization. Such is the power of relationships.

Nancy's story shared earlier is an example of the perks you can get through strong networking. But building relationships just for the sake of getting something in return would not get you anywhere. Remember, what goes around comes around.

SIX PILLARS OF A HEALTHY RELATIONSHIP

You agree that relationships are important and understand that you have to build good relationships. But how would you define a good relationship?

Any relationship requires six basic characteristics, which work together to make it strong and secure. Let's call them the pillars of a relationship, because when you lose even one, the relationship gets weaker.

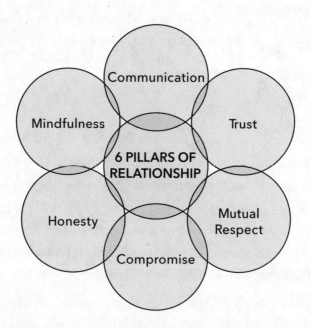

SIX PILLARS OF A GOOD RELATIONSHIP

1 *Communication*

All relationships depend on open communication. Trying to build a relationship without communication is like trying to travel by flight without a ticket. You will also find yourself in a similar no-entry situation if you are not ready to communicate. The more effective your communication, the richer will be your relationship.

2. *Trust*

No relationship can last without trust. Trust establishes a powerful bond between the people involved. When you trust the other person, you don't have to constantly watch your back; you can focus on the relationship. And trust has to be mutual. It's not enough if you trust the person involved; you have to make yourself trustworthy too. If the other person can't trust you, then they cannot be open or honest with you.

3. *Honesty*

The key to making yourself trustworthy is honesty. When you are honest, with nothing to hide, you gain people's trust. Dishonesty, on the other hand, engenders confusion and mistrust. Honesty is always the best policy.

4. *Compromise*

You cannot always win an argument; in fact, you need not. The best relationships have a foundation built on compromise. If you remain steadfast on always having your way, you better be a lone traveler. Even in your professional life, you should be open to others' ideas and opinions. This would lead to innovation and progress.

5. *Mutual Respect*

When you respect someone, you value his or her opinions, thoughts, and ideas. When you give respect, you get respect. This mutual respect would pave the way for a strong relationship. At work, mutual respect helps develop solutions with collective knowledge, ideas, and creativity.

6. *Mindfulness*

You have to take responsibility for your words and actions. You have to be attentive to what you say and take care that you don't make false promises and that you always keep your side of the deal. You also should be careful to not take your negative emotions out on other people.

Relationships take time and hard work.

INVEST IN GOOD RELATIONSHIPS

As we already saw, every relationship is unique. You can have several reasons for building relationships. However, in order to establish a relationship you have to devote your time. Relationships are like investments—the more you put in, the more you can get out of it.

Building relationships takes determination, perseverance, and hard work. And it's not easy if you are not ready to commit to the six pillars of relationship. A manager at the World Bank once said:

> *"Building relationships requires a thousand cups of tea."*

You should be willing to invest in what it takes in order to form a strong relationship.

Rohit was young entrepreneur. The success of his business had its foundations on networking. In the initial stages of his business, he used to be on the road meeting people and forming connections almost every day of the year. He worked hard. He never took a day off. You could even say he lived in his car. If, during one meeting, he received another contact, he would always be willing to go that extra mile, irrespective of the time of the day.

During one such house call, Rohit visited one of his Indonesian friends. After talking business, his friend invited him to join the family dinner. Being Indian, Rohit was not accustomed to Indonesian cuisine. However, he did not hesitate and joined his friend.

Even though this seems a simple and small thing, the willingness to adjust and adapt to any situation is a commendable quality. Had Rohit refused his friend's invitation, he would have lost his goodwill. His ability and readiness to adjust and adapt brought Rohit goodwill and made him very popular.

Building strong relationships takes this kind of commitment, dedication, and hard work. The people in the higher echelons of life have one thing in common—no matter what heights they reach, they do not shy away from expanding their professional contacts and friendships.

EIGHT GOLDEN RULES FOR PROFESSIONAL RELATIONSHIPS

In order to keep within the scope of the book, let's look at ways to build professional relationships. However, most of the ways given here are applicable to personal relationships as well.

1. Listen

Listening is the most crucial aspect of building relationships. Were you looking for something more complicated? Frankly, we all know that active listening is not very easy. However, it has great results.

When people know that you are truly listening and not just pretending to listen, they trust you more and communicate more freely with you. You may think, "When will I have the time to say what I want to say?" However, if you truly listen to people, they would actually want to know your opinions and insights.

Even if it's your show, don't monopolize; provide space for others to share. If they seem reluctant, be bold and encourage them to share their opinion. You will earn respect and trust when you truly listen. Nature has given us two ears and one mouth; let's use them in that proportion!

If people find that you are not really listening, they will either feel bad about themselves and withhold from sharing complete information or think that you are just wasting their time and refuse to meet you again.

When you listen actively to the other person, you genuinely show an interest in what the other person is saying. What more does a person want than to know that what he/she says is truly valued.

2 *Be a Giver*

Human beings are selfish by nature. Before getting into anything, we consciously or subconsciously ask ourselves, "What's in it for me?" If this is natural for you, then it's also natural for the person with whom you are trying to build a relationship.

When you are trying to establish a business relationship, before asking for something, offer something. More often than not, a genuine explanation for what you want or even your undivided attention is enough to build a rapport. This is where honesty comes into play.

The best relationships are mutually beneficial. People who have strong contacts always enter a relationship thinking about what they can give. Giving is the best way to ensure that you make a lasting connection.

If you approach the relationship thinking about the other person and not making it seem as if it's all about you, you make real connections in time. That's how you make friends.

3. Keep Your Word

When you promise something, make sure you keep it. Each time you break a promise, you are losing respect and trust. If you say you will do something, commit yourself to deliver your promise as promptly as you can, without their reminder. This would show them that you really mean what you say and that you respect them.

It is also important to learn to say no. When people ask for something that you know you will not be able to deliver, don't make false promises. Don't string them along. When you say you can help them, people want to believe you. Don't break that trust by giving false hopes. Remember the Golden Rule: *"Do unto others as you would have them do unto you."*

You don't like it when people make false promises, do you? And it feels really bad to go and ask someone again and again, doesn't it? So, don't do it to others. Moreover, people will respect you more when you are honest and say no.

4. Allocate Time

Schedule your day so that you have at least 20 minutes for relationship building. Twenty minutes may seem too much on a tight schedule. But if you break them into, say, five-minute segments, you can easily squeeze that in your day.

You don't even have to make face-to-face meetings every day. With LinkedIn, Twitter, and Facebook, you can make the most of your five-minute agenda and get in touch with multiple people in a day. Be sure to reply to people's postings and to return calls. Prompt replies and callbacks show that you are dependable.

If you do have time, then turn your coffee breaks and lunchtime into coffee meetings and lunch meetings. This can be an efficient use of your time. Besides, face-to-face meetings are much more effective than interactions over a phone or from behind a computer screen.

These little interactions can go a long way in establishing a strong connection.

5. Be Prepared

Many a times when people are given time, they hardly know what to say or where to begin. This is quite common and can happen to anyone. But it does not create a good impression. Moreover, you may get a chance to meet someone when you are least expecting it. It is always wise to be prepared.

How can you be prepared if you are not ready? Planning. Always make long-term plans and then break them down into short-term plans. Think big and you will go big. If you only make short-term plans, it will leave you unprepared and spoil your chances of meeting the person and his/her contacts ever again. Word of mouth is not very kind, especially when you are the subject.

Being prepared, on the other hand, creates a great first impression and improves your chances of turning the relationship into a long-lasting connection. Even if your meeting is planned, you may become tongue-tied in the moment if you have not prepared enough. Have a clear idea of what you are going to achieve by the end of the interaction and make sure you do. This would show the other person that you are not simply wasting their time and that the relationship is going to be productive.

6. *Genuinely Care*

Relationships can only be sustained if you show the other person that you are genuine in your interactions. No one wants to be a resource for someone else's consumption. Everyone is unique and wants to be known as a unique individual.

So, how do you show other people that you care for them? You can do that by simply paying attention to them. If Sid seems a little dull, ask after him. If you hear Mary is going on a vacation, make sure that you ask her about it the next time you meet her. Or perhaps you hear that Andrew's wife has had a baby; congratulate him and wish him luck when you see him. These small things matter most in a relationship.

For instance, if you performed a task for one of your colleagues, you can follow that up by sending an email or dropping by their office, saying, "Hope that worked for you," or "How did it turn out?" This shows your colleague that you care how things went for them and in turn makes your relationship stronger.

Also, you should clearly demarcate personal and professional life. Just because you bump into someone at the supermarket does not mean you can talk business. People shouldn't dread running into you. Respect their personal space.

7. Be Ready to Learn

You should never stop learning. If you are ready to be a student, life never stops teaching you. Nobody is perfect; each individual should have their own forte in which they are the king or the queen.

There are so many little things that add up to make a great relationship. Observe your colleagues and superiors in meetings or work-related interactions. When you are open to learning, you would be able to see everything differently—from a learning perspective. It would be like seeing through a different pair of eyes. Of course, you will see both positive and negative things. Put the negative aside. Focus on the positives.

What do your colleagues, superiors, or people you admire excel at? How differently do they handle a similar situation? What is their body language when they are interacting with someone? These insights will provide you constant ways to improve yourself and hence your relationships. Talk to people who you think have great contacts. Learn their process. It may be slightly different from yours.

Pick things up you like and ignore the rest. Constant learning has only one result—progress.

8. *Value the Message, but Also Value the Messenger*

It is easy to respect people and their ideas, inputs, and opinions when they are in the position of authority, power, or fame. You would probably be ready to put into practice the words of Warren Buffet, Bill Gates, or Ratan Tata. But what if you receive a great piece of advice from your gardener? The advice is great, but would you take it? Would you be even ready to listen to him?

If you are smart, you should. Great people strip away the prejudice that might come with a source and only look at the merit of the message. If an idea is good, they know it regardless of where it came from. Similarly, they also value good people, regardless of their perceived status.

Just because you heard it from a low-level employee, do not automatically dismiss an input or idea. Who knows, the idea might even get you out of your problem or be the turning point in your career.

WEEDING OUT CONFLICTS

It is normal in any relationship to have disagreements. But if you resolve the conflicts constructively, it will only strengthen your relationship. You may have to work with someone you don't like, can't relate to, or are not comfortable working with. This often happens in your professional life, but you cannot escape from them. Don't fear a conflict—face it.

Needless to say, engaging in an argument on who is right or wrong is not the best idea. American education reformist Horace Mann puts it brilliantly:

> *"Do not think of knocking out another person's brains because he differs in opinion from you. It would be as rational to knock yourself on the head because you differ from yourself ten years ago."*

When a conflict arises in your relationship, the ideal way would be to act professionally. Take a moment to analyze what caused the conflict. A conflict arises not because of the people involved but because of what they say. So, it's not the person with whom you are angry. You are angry at what he/she said. Can you spoil a relationship just based on what a person said? Is the one disagreement worth all the time you invested and all the hard work you went through to establish the relationship? Probably not. Like Mahatma Gandhi said:

> *"An eye for an eye will only make the whole world blind."*

Constructive conflict resolution strengthens your relationship.

Unless it involves unethical or illegal issues, no disagreement is worth a broken relationship. Once you realize this, you are halfway to resolving the conflict. After this, the other half is easy. This is where compromise plays a huge role.

Here is a step-by-step procedure to approach conflicts:

Step 1: Clarify the issue. Determine what exactly gave rise to the problem. List down where you agree and where you disagree. Clear this up with the other person involved. Only when you separate the non-issues can you concentrate on the issue at hand.

Step 2: Listen to what the other person has to say on the issue without interrupting or disagreeing outright. Understand her point of view. You may know that she is wrong, but only if you understand the why can you arrive at a compromise.

Step 3: Make the other person see your point of view. Because you first listened to her perspective, she will be more patient and willing to listen to yours. Don't be aggressive; just put your opinions and your reasons in a non-authoritative manner.

Step 4: Interact with the other person and work together to arrive at a win-win situation. You must also be open to the fact that a third option may be available. When you use this approach, you would see that an agreement surfaces on its own.

Following an organized method to conflict resolution helps you preserve and even strengthen your relationship.

More often than not, the other person may only be waiting for you take the first step. When you take the first step, you are recognized as the one who wants to maintain the relationship and that always works in your favor.

NOW FOR THE TOUGHEST PART

We now come to the final question. You have toiled hard, handled conflicts professionally, and established a relationship. How do you sustain it? To build a relationship takes some characteristics, whereas to sustain a relationship, it takes other, far difficult behavior traits.

Sustaining relationships is more challenging than building relationships.

1. Stepping in Without Being Asked To

Everyone helps when he/she is asked. But very few people offer assistance even before they are asked. When you pay close attention, you will be able to tell when a person is struggling and might do with an extra hand. It is at times like this that your assistance makes the greatest impact. This also shows that you truly care.

2. Taking the Hit

Some people have the courage to take the hit, irrespective of what the issue is or whose fault it is. People look up to such selfless individuals who are ready to accept the criticism or abuse. Such courage is always valued and makes the relationship stronger.

3. Knowing When to Dial It Down

Successful people have a great charisma, but they know when to show their individuality and when not to. In the event of a major setback or a highly stressful situation, you should focus on arriving at the solution by working together.

You should know when it is okay to have fun, when to be serious, when to lead, and when to follow.

4. Realizing and Accepting Your Mistakes

Responsibility is a crucial part of relationships. If you realize your mistakes and apologize for them before you are asked to or before anyone even notices, you earn respect and awe. Accepting and apologizing for your mistake can be one of the most difficult things that you have to do, especially if your subordinates are involved. However, this can prevent a mistake from being a permanent roadblock.

CHAPTER REWIND
CHAPTER REWIND

- Humans are essentially social by nature.

- Good relationships strengthen your mind and body and help improve your connection with others.

- Strong professional relationships provide you the opportunity for advancement in your career.

- Healthy personal relationships foster individual growth.

- Building relationships takes determination, perseverance, and hard work.

- Resolve disagreements and conflicts tactfully. View these as opportunities for preserving and even strengthening your relationships.

- While you build new relations, also focus on sustaining your existing relationships.

Chapter 8

Doing Things Differently

*"Words differently arranged
have a different meaning, and
meanings differently arranged
have different effects."*
—Blaise Pascal

SILLY PUTTY

Do you know Silly Putty? Do you know how it came into being? During World War II, there was a shortage of rubber. The government of the United States invited the industrialists to invent synthetic rubber to meet the shortage. General Electric (GE) created a substance called "gupp." It was interesting—it had amazing bouncy and stretchy properties, but it was not artificial rubber. Because of its interesting properties, GE sent out samples of gupp to scientists all over the world to come up with an application. But nothing happened.

One Peter Hodgson saw a toy store owner, Ruth Fallgatter, playing with gupp. They both thought that it would make a great toy. Next year, Hodgson borrowed $147 for buying gupp and its patent rights from GE. He gave it a funny name, used unique packaging, and displayed its new application as a toy—Silly Putty was born. Hodgson never had to worry about money anymore!

BUCKLE UP! BE DIFFERENT

Hodgson's story is what's called being different. The first requirement for having a new approach to what we do is to be creative. Everyone is creative. Each one of us has the potential to imagine and to create. Creativity is not an activity but a quality. Singing, painting, dancing, writing, and developing are not creative in themselves. We can paint or write in an uncreative way. We can also clean our closet in a creative way. We can bring creativity to any activity we are doing.

Creativity is the first step to being different.

When you bring in the factor of creativity, whatever you do stands out. Your work becomes different from what everyone else has been doing. And when you differentiate yourself from millions of similar people like you, you have accomplished success. It's true that success has a different meaning to everyone. But when you choose your path and start working toward your destination, you will find that you are not alone. There are thousands of people on the same path working toward a similar destination. This is where being different becomes important, crucial even. Once you establish yourself as different, you can draw your own path to your destination.

THE TWO VILLAGES OF ETHIOPIA

A bold experiment was carried out recently by a non-profit organization, One Laptop Per Child (OLPC). OLPC is involved in research for the creation of affordable educational devices for developing countries. Their aim is to reach the 100 million first-grade-aged children worldwide who do not have access to schooling or education.

In 2012, OLPC tried something new in two villages in Ethiopia. They simply dropped off boxes of tablets with pre-loaded educational programs. These boxes were sealed shut, with no instructions of any sort. The villages chosen were so remote and rural that children there had never previously seen any printed material—no road signs, not even packaging that had words on it!

The tablets were solar powered. Ethiopian technicians had taught the adults in the village to use the solar charging system. Once a week, a technician went to the village and swapped the memory card in the tablets to study how the tablets had been used. The objective of this experiment was to see if illiterate kids, with no prior exposure to written words, could learn to read by themselves with the help of the alphabet-training programs loaded on the tablets. What do you think might have happened?

Nicholas Negroponte, the founder of OLPC, said that he had expected the kids to play with the boxes. However, within four minutes, one of the kids had not only opened the box, but had also found the power button and had switched the tablet on. Remember, these kids had never seen a power button before in their life. Within five days, the kids were using an average of 47 apps per child per day. Within two weeks, the kids were singing ABC songs in English, and within five months they had hacked Android! Can you believe that?

And it did not stop with that. OLPC's chief technology officer said that they had installed a software in the tablets to freeze desktop settings, so that they could not be customized. However, the kids had found a way to work around that and had completely customized the desktops—every kid's desktop looked different! Kids were even learning to write with the help of the literacy apps in the tablets. They had been found to use paint programs to spell words and to arrange jumbled letters to form words.

These children, who had never seen written words before in any language, had learned to read and write all by themselves! People involved in this project have been overwhelmed at this result. OLPC has proposed to continue this research to find conclusive and scientific results.

If those children in isolated, remote villages of the world have the potential to use their creativity to teach themselves a completely new language, don't you think you have the potential to be creative and different too?

YOU'RE BORN DIFFERENT

How many people you have met look exactly like you? How many people you know think like you? Nature intends us to be different. This is why we rarely see people who look like us, think like us, have the same approach to life, have similar likes, dislikes, and priorities in life. So, in a way, you are already different. You just have to be different in the things you do. To do things differently, you have to use a little bit of your creativity.

**Creativity is not an activity.
It's an attitude.**

Creativity does not mean that you come up with great new ideas every time you are in a difficult situation. It's just an attitude—it's how you look at your situation. You don't need an innovative perspective; you just need a different perspective—one that no one has thought of and one that others have discarded or ignored.

Every problem has not one but multiple solutions. You just have to remember this. In a situation, if you remember that you have multiple solutions available, you force yourself to think about all of them. This way, you force yourself to think creatively. But if you think there is only one solution, then you are quenching your creativity and submitting to being ordinary.

A study indicates that around 95 percent of children between ages three and five are highly creative. But when the same children are tested as teenagers, only 5 percent are found to be highly creative. So what happened in between? Do we lose our ability to think creatively when we grow up? No. This is the result of teaching children to stop being creative!

Children have the tendency to ask a lot of questions— why, why not, how, so what, and what if? They also come up with the strangest ideas and fantasies. But as they grow up and start school, this tendency is often discouraged. If any of their ideas challenge the teacher or the system, they are simply silenced. They are given the answer, "That's how it is and that's how it should be." They are told that to get along in this world, they will have to go along with others. Finding no outlet and in order to be liked and accepted by peers, they curb their creativity and put it to hibernate.

They learn to see the world the way they are taught. They stop questioning and start following. They start seeing answers as right or wrong. They don't analyze why it is so. They eliminate what they consider wrong by default. This narrows the solutions available to them. They forget to exercise creativity, to see things in a different light. Then they despair that their problems are too big, that they don't have any solution, and that they will never be able to achieve success.

By nature, all of us have the potential to be creative. But by following others blindly and abandoning our natural tendency to question, we stop being creative. As Robert Frost said in his poem "The Road Not Taken," we don't always have to follow our peers blindly. In fact, we shouldn't. Instead, we can learn from them and use this knowledge to build our own path. Not everything in life is right or wrong. Life is way too ambiguous for that. Choose the road that is less trodden like Frost says and that will truly make all the difference:

> *"Two roads diverged in a wood, and I,*
> *I took the one less travelled by,*
> *And that has made all the difference."*

LOOK OUT! SOME HABITS CAN QUELL CREATIVITY

Because each of us is born to be different, it is the habits we inculcate during our lives that stop us from being creative. Let us now look closely at the common habits people have that quell their creativity.

1. *Fear of Change*

Most people hate change. They refuse to accept change. Some are even scared of change. By rejecting change, you are only preventing progress. Change is highly essential for any creative process because the process itself involves change. By being creative, you are forcing yourself to change your approach and use a different approach to your situation. So, if you rebel against change, you prevent yourself from viewing things in a different perspective, and hence you are trampling your creativity.

2. Fear of Being Wrong

Years and years of school education has taught us the concept of right and wrong and that being wrong is bad. So it is understandable that you are afraid of being wrong and making mistakes. However, this fear would forever prevent you from doing anything. The worst and the best thing about making mistakes is the experience that you learn from them. When you are scared of the outcome, you cannot focus on the process. This is why fear of being wrong quenches creativity, where there is no right or wrong.

3. Perfectionism

This is one step ahead of being scared of making mistakes. When you are a perfectionist, you expect nothing but the right, nothing but the best from yourself. But sadly, nobody can be perfect. You put yourself under pressure when you expect to do things that you consider right. When you fall short, you are highly disappointed in yourself. A perfectionist attitude prevents you from approaching any problem differently because you don't want to fail.

4. Pessimism

If you think you cannot be creative, you prevent yourself from being creative. You fulfill your self-made prophecy. This is because, when you think you are not creative, you draw an imaginary box around yourself and avoid stepping out of it. You accept that you cannot be creative and thus prevent yourself from indulging in creative thinking.

5. Lack of Confidence

This is similar to the pessimistic attitude. When you lack self-confidence, you don't believe in your abilities. Even if you come up with new ideas, you reject them thinking that you can never get it right. Sometimes, when you make mistakes or your idea fails, you lose further confidence in yourself and stop believing in your abilities. This puts a lid on your creativity.

If you recognize any of these unhealthy habits in yourself, you know what's stopping you from being creative. Start working on losing these habits. Here are a few tips:

1. Welcome change, for change is the only thing that is permanent. Remember, whatever you do, you are not going to remain the same. Besides, not all change is bad. Creative thinking is one such change that will transform you for good. One way to reduce the impact of change is to introduce it gradually.

2. Embrace failure. Failure is a better teacher than success. Don't be scared to make mistakes.

Like Amos Bronson Alcott said: *"Our bravest and best lessons are not learned through success, but through misadventure."*

3. Accept that not everyone is perfect. This doesn't mean that you shouldn't set high standards for yourself. It's okay if you don't come up to your standards all the time. This would allow you to try different approaches. If one doesn't work out, there is always another solution.

4. Regulate your thoughts. Negative thinking is easy to control once you know your thoughts. Whenever you find you have a negative one lurking, weed it out with a stronger, positive thought. Once you start nurturing positive thoughts and ignoring negative ones, you will see pessimism fade away gradually.

5. Understand the process. Some of your thoughts may seem crazy at first, some may fail, but when you understand that failure is inevitable and nothing is impossible, you start building confidence. Don't get disappointed when one of your approaches doesn't yield what you expected, and don't forget to celebrate when you come up with a solution for a particularly difficult situation.

Start incorporating the habits mentioned above instead of the unhealthy habits, and before you know it you will be able to see both the sides of the coin.

CREATIVITY FOR SUCCESS

"Happiness is not in the mere possession of money; it lies in the joy of achievement, in the thrill of creative effort."
—FRANKLIN D. ROOSEVELT

People often ask, "What are my chances of making it big?" This is an unfair question. Imagine this—if you enrolled for the same program at the same fitness center where Hugh Jackman works out, what would be your chances of looking like him? This entirely depends on the effort you put in for your workouts. Similarly, the probability of your success is proportional to your efforts. The right question to ask then is, "What is the level of success that would satisfy me?" When you have the answer in mind, keep that as your target and start working toward it.

We don't fall into the habit of winning until we start doing our work. Life is not about guarantees or securities; life is about the freedom to succeed and the freedom to fail. It is about imagining the big picture and working hard toward it.

Creativity is one of the essential components of success. If you achieve something that a thousand others have achieved before, it is not called success. Imagine you are a high school student in a math class. Your teacher gives you an assignment problem on the method you were taught today. All your friends follow the method your teacher taught to solve the problem. But you use a different method. It doesn't even have to be a new one; let's say you solve the problem using a method you were taught a couple of years ago. The solution you arrive at is the same as the one that your friends arrive at. However, your method takes fewer steps to arrive at the solution. Wouldn't you feel elated at having used the different method? Now, this is success.

Everyone faces challenges on the path to success. You cannot succeed without overcoming challenges. Henry Ford had to do it, Bill Gates had to do it, you would have to do it too. What challenges do you think you would have to deal with? Don't be discouraged by them; instead, face them.

You might look at someone with financial resources and think, "Hey, he can do this because he has money." But look closely—he might not have the health to support his efforts. Or someone else might have the health and the money, but might have a relationship problem at home, which would prevent him from enjoying the fruits of his labor. Look around—nobody is free of challenges. What makes you a winner is your ability to overcome these challenges.

Leverage your creativity. It will take you to your success.

Use your creativity as a weapon to conquer your challenges. A different perspective would allow you to see the challenge in a different light. This would open up multiple ways to rise above your challenges.

Dare to be different. Keep thinking of different ways to solve a problem. Consider all the solutions you find; don't discard any. If you find a path that no one has chosen before, do not be afraid to try it. Creativity is the one instrument that will allow you to make your own path when you can't find the path.

Before we close, let's summarize the attributes of attitude. Write them and put them in a place where you see them daily. Let these guiding lights take you to your destiny. *Bon voyage!*

THE RIGHT ATTITUDE

- Never stop dreaming. Never stop turning your dreams into goals.

- Be optimistic.

- You can. You can. You will.

- Believe in your ideas.

- Be determined. Stay determined.

- Work your passion.

- Build honest relationships.

- Dare to be different.